Connecticut Shore Line

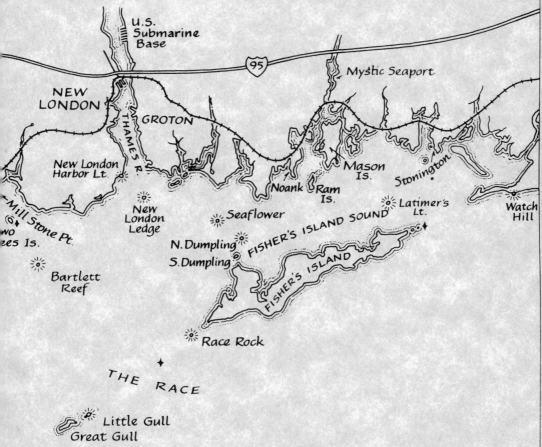

U.S.
Submarine
Base

95

Mystic Seaport

NEW
LONDON

GROTON

THAMES R.

New London
Harbor Lt.

Mason
Is.

Noank   Ram
Is.

Stonington

New
London
Ledge

Seaflower

Latimer's
Lt.

Mill Stone Pt.

wo
es Is.

FISHER'S ISLAND SOUND

Watch
Hill

Bartlett
Reef

N. Dumpling

S. Dumpling

FISHER'S ISLAND

Race Rock

THE RACE

Little Gull
Great Gull

ATLANTIC OCEAN

Christmas 2003

For Joe Denhart:
May you always have a fair breeze
and a following tide!

BLUEBERRY
A Boat of the Connecticut Shoreline

David D. Hume

J.N. TOWNSEND PUBLISHING
EXETER, NEW HAMPSHIRE
1994

Cartography by R. P. Hale.

Typography by Bert Clarke.

Printed by BookCrafters.
Second Edition, 1995.

Published by
J. N. Townsend Publishing
12 Greenleaf Drive
Exeter, New Hampshire 03833
(603) 778-9883

Text and display type were set in Janson Text,
using Macintoch PageMaker v. 5.0.

LIBRARY OF CONGRESS CATALOGING-IN-PUBLICATION DATA

Hume, David D.
    Blueberry / by David D. Hume.
        p. cm.
    ISBN 1-880158-02-7 : $22.50
    1. Blueberry (Sailboat) 2.Boats and boating—
United States. 3. Boatbuilding—United
                States. I. Title

796. 1'24--DC20   93-29842
                                              CIP

Foreword

This book was written for the pleasure of reliving some sailing adventures with *Blueberry* during the winter months when she is on the shore under her plastic counterpane. But building the boat and participating in her design were other sorts of pleasure that also merited vicarious repetition and so the text grew to encompass a number of things. One result of this has been the inclusion of a lot of nautical terminology that will not, I hope, put off the general reader. To help out I have included a brief glossary of terms on page 104.

Acknowledgments

I am grateful to Sigmund Diamond and Edmund Delaney for urging me to get on with the discipline of writing. Edmund was also an initial cause of much of what follows by towing that leaking old Penguin Dinghy up the length of Long Island Sound behind his ancient ketch *Sabrina* and presenting it to me, free and clear, thirty years ago. My cousin Tom Hume added much to my nautical education. My brother Michael made sensible suggestions for additions and explanations in this text. Cathy Hume, best and dearest critic, has suffered the piercing shriek of the dot matrix printer during the composition of this and read the resulting manuscript many more times than mere pleasure would prompt, mostly in a relentless quest to correct a congenitally inventive orthography that not even the word processor could master. But most of the credit and none of the blame for what is here must go to Phil Bolger. Our correspondence has been a delight to me and his permission to reproduce much of it here is a characteristic act of generosity on his part. He gives me more than enough credit for my part in the design of *Blueberry*; he created her out of the amateur sketches of an untrained enthusiast and cheered me on during those extended years of construction. Finally, first books, like first boats also require expert design to turn out well. Bert Clarke encouraged me from the start and designed this book for friendship's sake. Sadly, he did not live to see it off the press.

D.D.H.
Salem, Connecticut and
Wilmington, North Carolina
1993

I. *Solo September Cruise*

Sometimes it seems forever before the tide turns the current in the Connecticut River. I had waited until after one PM before leaving Hamburg Cove in the expectation that I would get a rapid ride down past Essex to Saybrook light, but the buoys were still leaning upriver as I approached the Baldwin Bridge and the wind had gone fitful and fluky in the west. When I left the Cove the tide seemed full and the grassy inlet where the Eight Mile River meets the Connecticut was full to the brim. The usual resident pair of great blue heron were elsewhere, presumably poking into shallower waters, and the local swans were dabbling at the point where the Outer Cove narrows down to the eastern channel that runs from the flat half tide rock north past the older houses among the hemlocks and maples.

It is sad to see the hemlocks turning grey and dry as the blight takes them, a few more each year. Soon they will all be gone. Along this shore houseowners are planting deciduous trees and there are a few white pines coming in. I wish people would plant fewer white pines, especially the Department of Transportation which has been decorating the approaches of rebuilt bridges with them. In two year's time they make the view of the water quite invisible from the road. Soon driving through rural Connecticut will be like passing through a green tunnel as the unprofitability of small farms encourages less open land and we become a sort of replacement for the threatened Brazilian rain forest. All the views of the famed American Impressionist painters around Old Lyme are already invisible. The glimpses from the highways are disappearing fast.

The morning had started sunny and windless in the Inner Cove. I got away from the dock to the comfortable muttering of the little diesel in *Blueberry*'s belly. As I motored down the length of the cove I set up the Autohelm to keep me in the channel, although almost any place in Hamburg is adequate for our 2'10" draft if the tide is full. With the little black box minding the helm I set the staysail, peaked up the main with the weight of the boom still on the topping lift, and then let it settle to take the wrinkle out of the sail. In the Outer Cove we passed Jim Raftery's lovely schooner *Golden Goose* and Bob Baumer's *Gjoa* before we made the turn out to the west.

I cut the red nun on the south side of the mouth of the Cove and tried to lay a tack to clear the green daymarker #29 at the south end of Brockway Island. No luck. Wind to south of west and the tide still hindering the tacks down river. The tower and concrete base of the daymarker supported their usual population of cormorants and a few more besides. Two were up at the light on the top, just above the big bundle of sticks that marked the osprey nest. The osprey were obviously not at home today. The cormorants yielded possession of the top of the tower when they were.

I powered down towards Ely's Ferry, shut down the diesel and surveyed the river. There was only one other boat underway. Tuesdays are better than weekends on the Connecticut in late summer. My companion turned out to be a battered Brockway skiff with an ancient Evinrude on his transom. He was trailing a fishing line in the swirl of the still rising tide north of the marker. There were a few high cirrus clouds in the west and a clear straight contrail pointing to the southwest towards Kennedy airport a hundred miles beyond my horizon. I could barely see his silver triangular shape leading the white pencil lines of his trail. I'm sure he couldn't see me, although even from 30,000 feet he had a great view of the river, the scrawl of Lord Cove, the north and south coves of Saybrook and Essex, the islands of the lower river: Great, Goose, Nott, Brockway, Calves and Eustasia. He had outdone the full three days of my planned voyage in the last five minutes.

I took a flat tack towards the Essex shore and rolled out the big jib with a satisfying *whump* as the wind filled it. It sets flying on its roller at the end of the flat fingered bowsprit that Phil Bolger had designed. *Blueberry* made a nice surge forward and leaned off the breeze. When the depth sounder read ten feet I tacked again and headed back to the east. That side of the river is the deeper and I still had thirty-eight feet when I was almost to the rock ledges under the trees along the shore. I tacked just a few yards from them.

With jib, staysail, and main all pulling, *Blueberry* can get up to better than five knots in a middling light air, but the tide was still besting the current by a couple of knots and the wide flat tacks I was making didn't get me down past Essex until after 2:00 PM. Passing the old Steamboat Dock, now the Connecticut River Museum, the wind shifted into the

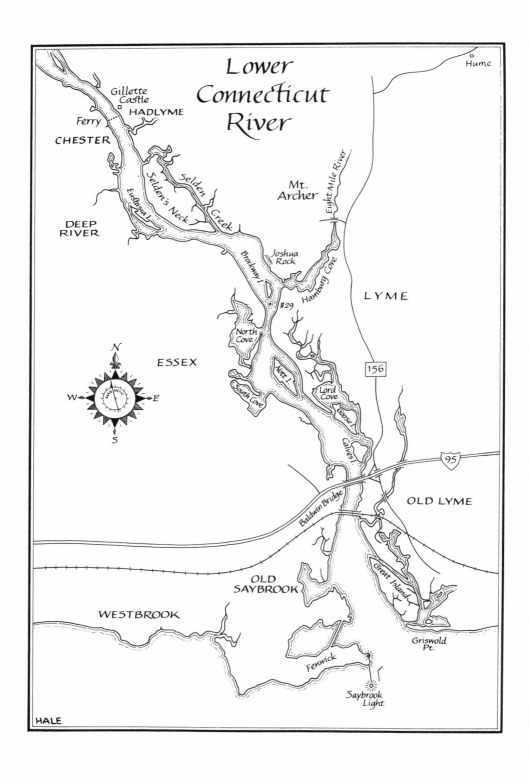

west and I eased off the sheets of all three sails on a south-easterly heading for the lower part of the river. A private dock with the British Union Jack flying was just off to starboard of my course. I shaved by the wrong side of the nun that marks the Nott Island shoal, taking advantage of my meager draft and the full tide. As I passed the nun the meter read 5.1 feet, three feet of which was the midday flood.

The long twisting point of land that separates Lord Cove from the river is decorated by one shingled cabin, itself sentineled by a rakishly skewed flag pole flying a pale, horizontally segmented American flag. I've never seen any-one about the place and today was no exception, but the flag has a touch of presence about it, even if it flies day and night in any weather.

The old Baldwin Bridge is being replaced by something that looks from beneath like a pair of sleek toothpaste extrusions done in concrete. They already span the river between Old Lyme and Old Saybrook so that just now there are three bridges, all with vertical clearance of better than sixty feet. Underneath there is a burgeoning forest of gigan-tic concrete pillars set on granite-cased bases. The tide swirls around them and the wind drops sharply as you pass among them. A boost with the diesel seemed appropriate. Beyond the highway bridges, there is a stretch of open river north of the much lower railroad bridge. Here there is room to tack and jill about waiting for the draw to open. Today was almost clear sailing, but the bridge started slowly down while I was still a quarter of a mile short of the gap. I switched the VHF to channel 13 on a polite low power of one watt and summoned the attention of the "Old Lyme Draw," an-nouncing that I was *Blueberry* requesting the time of your next opening."

"This is Old Lyme Draw. Where are you now, Cap'n; how far are you?"

I suddenly had an image of him peering alternately up and

down the river from his elevated cabin among the bridge girders, trying to discern a 200-foot oil barge and pushing tug coming down from Hartford or in from Long Island Sound. Those tows have a huge momentum and would need a couple of miles to stop if the bridge was to stay closed in front of them.

"I'm the little gaff cutter about 300 yards north of you," I answered.

There was a brief silence. I began to wonder if he thought I could squeak under the closed span in spite of *Blueberry's* 20-foot mast and high peaked gaff that reached above the navigational and strobe lantern at the truck. I reflected that I really had never figured out just how high the tip of the raised gaff was from the waterline.

"It'll be about twelve minutes, Captain," spoke the metallic voice of the radio

I thanked the Old Lyme Draw and switched back to the dual watch of channels Nine and Sixteen that has become the standard for VHF communication. Sixteen is now meant to be reserved for emergencies only and the usual boat traffic calling channel has become Nine. When cruising single-handed, being alone is not at all lonely, but hearing the communication in the neighborhood is a pleasant sort of company and an occasional word with a bridge keeper is a memorable event of sociability.

I was joined by a sport fisherman with a high tuna tower and a white yawl with her sail covers buttoned on. They drifted in the slack water while I circled between the banks for ten minutes until there was a husky hoot and a deep grumble from the huge ancient bridge machinery. I touched the start button and went through the gap under power. Massive timbering protecting the stone abutments of the bridge on both sides shows signs of rough contact with vessels of much larger size than mine. I wonder how many of the tugs bashed into the timbers and just rammed their barges through, tearing off a few pieces of 12 x 12 tarred fir in the process.

The southwest afternoon onshore breeze favored long tacks down the river and short ones across it to get out to the breakwaters and the two lighthouses at Saybrook Point. Progress was slow, in spite of the fact that the tide had finally turned in our favor. The charts below the bridges are in the 1 to 40,000 scale and the location of the subsurface piles and shoals are hard to estimate. A shadowy presence of something called "Sodom Rock" is somewhere to the near east side of the buoyed channel. The implied discomfort of its title is enough to keep most boats to the west of the red markers, but I saw a couple of planing motor boats, Bayliners I thought, skimming by its presumed location. After a while I cast discretion to the wind and bore off past Griswold Point to the southeast with a nervous eye on the digits of the depth meter. It rapidly dropped to two feet and then for a moment showed a horrifying 1.8 in between a couple of 2.0s. The sounder's transducer is well over a foot below the load water line, but one and six tenths feet on the meter should be hard aground. With the tide at the full flood, going aground on

the bar at Saybrook in the late afternoon is a lousy idea. I resolved not to cut the easterly channel so fine again.

But the bar at the mouth of the river, between Old Saybrook and Old Lyme, has in the long run been a friend to the yachtsman. From the time that Adrien Block sailed his Manhattan-built *Onrust* up Long Island Sound and explored the lower Connecticut valley in 1614, all have agreed with him that the lower stretch of the river was "very shallow". Until late in the Nineteenth Century, it remained too shallow for a deep water seaport and too wide to bridge. As a result the principal cities of Connecticut grew at New London on the Thames, at Hartford, well up the valley, and in the other towns to the west that were blessed with the natural resource of a roadstead such as Norwalk and Bridge-port. Boats and even quite sizable ships were built in Essex, but they had to be floated down river without ballast, guns, or spars, hoisted over the bar with "camels" or pontoons and towed to New London or Noank to receive the rest of their equipment. Nineteenth-century charts show a zigzag channel that could be threaded by vessels of less than ten-foot draft with local knowledge, but busy cities and seaports never developed along these banks. In recent times a dredged fairway between stone jetties leads the tugs and oil barges into this inland waterway to the very center of New England. But the shores of the lower valley are still unblemished by industrial development or even, for the most part, by railroad tracks along the river. Would that the Thames had been so spared. Much of the valley shore line has been protected as park land in recent years, although a few dozen large palazzi of the Era of Deregulation now squat where even a few years ago there was woodland, meadow, marsh and high rocky shore. Most of these new oversized houses are decorated with identical arched but un-palladian windows of great size, suggesting that the architects all shopped out of the same Peachtree or Anderson catalogues for their fenestration. They bring a whiff of Boca Raton or Key Biscayne to the "land of steady habits." They seem not to be grounded in the local sense of place. Come to think of it, Palladio himself got his commissions from nouveaux riches mercenary captains that made a buck or a ducat out of protecting the Signori of Venice. They retired to country farms but needed an architect with the chutzpa to make them look like nobility by the elegance of his line and the orders of his columns. Stanford White did the same thing for the railroad barons of the late nineteenth century. I guess the only difference is that Andrea and Stanford were much better architects and their clients were proportionately a hell of a lot richer than the hotshot investment bankers and leveraged buy-out operators of the 1980s.

But all those houses are back up the river from the mouth. There was very little undeveloped land for them down here. Beside me now were the little beach cottages of Old Lyme Shores, and astern I could see a few of the middle-sized, comfortable, shingle-style homes of Fenwick. I wonder at the future of some of the new homes. A couple of them are currently in the hands of the Resolution Trust since their owner's or builder's bankruptcies took several of the local lending institutions down with them. A mile to the west stands a grinning stone castle on Cornfield Point that would seem to be a pre-1929 version of the same sort of overblown architecture that afflicted the 1980s. It is used today as a Neapolitan seafood restaurant and steakhouse.

The wind had dropped to ten to twelve in the south west and the hour had gotten past four o'clock, 1600 hours in nautical time, but I was well off the Lyme shoals now and able to set a course of 100° Magnetic for the south tip of Black Point. But the wind dropped still more and by 1700 I was

under power, amusing myself by punching a new waypoint
into the Loran and wondering if I should have to spend the
night in the Niantic River rather than farther east.

But the tide was running a couple of knots in my favor and
in spite of being deserted by the wind, 6 PM found me south
of Goshen Point, making the turn to the northeast past the
Harkness Park and the white sand of Ocean Beach Park with
its attendant offshore rocks. The great square buildings of
the Millstone atomic power plant glowed pink in the late sun
over my left shoulder. I had three quarters of an hour of
September daylight left to get up into New London and find
an anchorage for the night. The four Pfizer stacks and the
confusion of pea green sheds and rust red lumps of the
General Dynamics Electric Boat Company emphasized the
differences between the Thames and Connecticut Rivers. I
powered slowly through the anchorage at Green's Harbor
and finally dropped the big (11 pound) Bruce anchor between two moored sailboats just under the protruding stone
bulkhead of the US Navy Underwater Sound Laboratories.
A great grey arch of a magnetic field producing gadget of
huge proportion loomed above me.

I lighted cabin and anchor lights, put Murray Periah's tape
of Mozart's 16th Piano Concerto on the boom box, broke
out a package of nacho chips and made a martini on the
rocks. The usual caveats about drinking alone don't seem to
me to apply to singlehanded sailing when one is anchored for
the night. Besides, *Blueberry* is a cheerful and communicative
companion in herself.

I had started drawing a cartoon for *Blueberry* more than a
dozen years earlier, hardly even believing that I would ever
actually build such a boat. But the fascination of trying to fit
the ideal accommodation for a singlehander into a twenty
foot sloop led me on. I drew a gaff rig to avoid the need for
a spinnaker to give her downwind power. The shoal draft

was for the Connecticut River, as was the self-tending staysail, to make short river tacks simple. The inboard ten horsepower diesel was my reply to years of winding a rope around the flywheel of the old British Seagull while drifting backwards in the tide toward some low bridge or shoal. A pair of batteries to use in alternation for a reliable start in the morning and a locker for a removable Coleman "Oscar" as a rot and mold-proof ice box were interior design elements garnered from experience.

The Seacook stove set my supper of tinned enchiladas bubbling in the pan. Served with sliced tomatoes, bread-sticks, cottage cheese and a beer, this makes an acceptable supper if you are hungry enough. I had a ripe nectarine and a couple of oatmeal cookies for dessert.

Blueberry carries a condensed library of some thirty or forty books, but sleep and waking on a boat are closely governed by the daylight and the dark and I was unable to stay with Prescott's *Conquest of Mexico* for very long. Rolling from the harbor traffic was minimal and I slept well enough for the first night out. Anyone on a cruise has discovered that the second night in the bunk of a small boat is more soporific than the first, but I had no trouble getting to sleep.

Morning came up pink with some mist, the surface of the harbor slick and glassy. To the south, Fisher's Island Sound was grey with an off shore fog. I had breakfast and mopped up the dew in the cockpit with the big bailing sponge. I decided to explore for a bit up the Thames before setting out for Mystic to the east. Despite some dire comments about the foul state of the bottom near my anchorage, the Bruce came up easily and clean. I powered over to the east shore, properly the city of Groton, and went up past Electric Boat. Up on the ways there was a huge rust colored shape with uss RHODE ISLAND painted on its side in disproportionately small letters. I don't know if it will be a Trident or a Seawolf, but it looks enormous from the water. I passed on and recrossed the river to the town dock by the railroad station. Union Station in New London is one of Henry Hobson Richardson's early great buildings. Its impressive bulk stands alone next to the water across the tracks, looking very modern in its shape. His library up at the other end of State Street is less successful, but for railroad stations, I'll take Richardson over White or Palladio any time.

I turned in towards the city marina and noted a good gathering of men fishing from the dock. They weren't catching anything that I could see and they looked as innocent of employment as I, but much less contented to be so.

New London and Groton are on hard chances now. Their economy is dominated by the Navy, the Coast Guard and the submarine industry. General Dynamics has stolidly refused to make any attempt to retool even a portion of Electric Boat and convert to some new non-bellicose form of industry, preferring to use surplus capital to bid up the price of their own stock. This keeps the shareholders happy and thus the management in their seats, but it does nothing for the out of work men fishing on the dock on a weekday morning.

As I repassed the huge shipyard on my way back down the river, it seemed to me that the place had a slack and discouraged look even where ships were actually being built. A few men moved about slowly among the rusting shapes and metal scaffolding of the ways, but there was very little movement in the yards and only one blue-flickering welder's spark showing from my vantage point. Maybe there is a lot of work going on inside the giant green sheds or in the interior of the partially completed *Rhode Island*. But if the exterior of the hull is finished now (and no one seems to be working further on it), I wondered why they don't give it a coat of paint. Possibly it is made of that steel-cum-copper alloy that is protected by its own coating of rust. Anyway, it looks as though things are winding down in Groton.

But then, as I headed down the channel, I saw a tall black tower atop a wrinkle in the glassy surface of the water that merged into the grey fog to the south. A modern submarine on the surface really doesn't produce any bow wave at all, just a gentle lumping up of the water at the sloping front of its nearly awash deck. Most of the great beast is invisible anyway, just twenty yards of rounded deck fore and aft of the sail and a slender black fin projecting from the water astern. An ensign on a portable flagstaff had been affixed to the aft end of the conning tower and three men were visible on the flying bridge. Another four crew members stood about on the deck aft. No one appeared to be doing much of anything and they studiously ignored the twenty-foot gaff cutter on their starboard hand. *Blueberry* is seldom ignored by other vessels. Bow-spritted gaffers of our size with coal-scuttle deck houses, handkerchief-sized forestaysails, lazy jacks, runners and the like are unusual enough to require a glance or a wave, sometimes even an approving hand signal or thumbs up, and even on occasion a dive to the cabin to bring up the camera. Not the submariners. All stared straight upriver and though they passed about a hundred feet away, I detected no smile. I waved cheerily anyway. Their ship looked trim and quite able, made no wake to disturb my morning, and even gave promise that the rusty leviathans on the beach at Electric Boat might someday look ship-shape in their turn.

The seriousness of the submarine's crew looked like the sort of thing one might expect on a training mission out of the big Navy Sub Base at Gales Ferry, up the Thames. At least they didn't look as though they were returning from a three month stay under the polar ice cap; no signs of anticipation, much less of jubilation among the riders of that black cigar.

An hour later I was sailing slowly before the wind off

Groton Long Point watching the line of bearing on the Seaflower light tower intersect with North Dumpling. Progress was slow, but the hour was early and the temperature pleasant. My goal had been defined as the 1215 opening on the Mystic River where Route US One crosses a splendid old bascule bridge between ice cream parlors, lemonade stands, pizza houses and other delicious accoutrements of a good tourist town.

I switched the tiny Loran over to the Course/Speed readout and eventually got a fairly consistent figure of 2.5 knots to the east. Considering a knot and half tide running against me, that worked out to something like four knots through the water which is about what it felt like. The breeze from the southwest had picked up a bit and, as always, my spirits improved with the wind. The day was a hazy sunny one. Public Radio was providing me J. S. Bach's Suite #3. A couple of small aircraft were practicing landing patterns at the Groton-New London Airport just north of me. Bach was occasionally interrupted by the VHF rasping out Coast Guard reports of people in trouble. A Hobie Cat with two aboard was overdue since last night outside of Buzzards Bay, south of Westport Massachusetts. A forty foot power boat was burning in the water some ten miles south of Montauk. I was glad to be happily coming up towards Noank. One of the big party schooners out of Mystic passed me on its tourist trip out into Fisher's Island Sound. He was pursued by a launch, hove to for a moment, and then resumed his direction. I think he took on a late passenger.

Coming up towards Noank I passed Abbott's where the lobsters are served to be eaten at picnic tables along the dock front. The wind was fair for threading up the Mystic anchorage, around its various turns until the span of the railroad swing bridge was in sight. I came around south, into the wind, set up the autohelm, put the engine at idle, and dropped the sails to wait for the opening. The railroad span opened soon enough, but just as I was congratulating myself on perfect timing, I came up to the Route One bridge under power and was able to read the clearly lettered sign stating that the bridge opened at 15 minutes past the hours from 7 AM to 6 PM *except* at 1215! I pulled over to the east shore of the channel where there was an unoccupied space at the dock next to a newly opened lemonade stand. The owner, a pleasant woman, provided me with a large cup of slush ice lemonade and an oddly colored hot dog with mustard but no sauerkraut. With better than an hour to kill, I explored downtown Mystic in search of another roll of film.

Mystic is a tourist town that is also a pleasant place to live, especially in the off-season. There are lots of city people with Bermuda length shorts and black ankle socks in the streets all summer long, their daughters in tight bicycle pants trimmed with a couple of inches of lace at mid-thigh. Their sons wear drooping khaki shorts above aggressively black, disproportionately large, high topped basketball sneakers, usually not fastened or tied. They walk with a sort of stoop and shuffle, as though they were a little embarrassed at being related to their parents, or perhaps even to themselves. Late childhood is a miserable time. I felt like hugging a couple of the boys around the shoulders and telling them that things would get better in a few years. The girls seemed to be having more uninhibited fun just now.

The dock mistress on duty at the Mystic Seaport waved me into a slip among a number of those vacant at this season of the year. I tied up, flemished down sheets and halyards in case any tourists happened by to admire her, and left Blueberry to walk up past the shipyard into the Seaport Museum proper.

There are enough things going on at the Mystic Seaport so that it is sometimes hard to figure out just what the place is meant to be. It is a costumed mid-nineteenth century replica of a New England town filled with real boats and a good number of real houses, although a few are reproductions. It also sells lemonade, but from an older formula than the lady's down by the bridge. But the Seaport is also a museum and the staff has a passionate attachment to authenticity of material and design. Boats being built in the boat shop are done in old materials: that is there is no plywood in sight, but I suspect that some modern glues are occasionally used and a lot of the tools are shining examples of the newest power equipment. The style of dress on the young concessionaires is nicely from the 1840s, the period of the flagship of Mystic, the *Charles W. Morgan*. But some of the best small boats in the collection are Herreshoffs of the early part of this century and the second best vessel in the fleet, the *L.A.Dunton*, was launched in 1921. I confess to being nonpurist in my approach to such things and I rather liked the ungleaned attic quality of the Seaport a few years ago. I don't mourn the removal of the Japanese midget submarine found originally in Pearl Harbor, but the lifeboat in which some impossible number of survivors had spent two or three months at sea was one of my favorites. They are currently sawing off the "pinkie" stern of a wooden boat because the vessel didn't have such originally. It was remodeled forty or fifty years ago, a discovery that was only made after the boat had been in the Seaport collection for several decades. I suppose that with the space for exhibiting things being limited, the most authentic should be shown to the public. The steel-hulled *Joseph Conrad* was originally called something else, but she made a romantic cruise under Allan Villiers and the earlier name was less illustrious and Danish, so the name plate hasn't been restored. The blacksmith hasn't taken to forging authentic toggle-headed harpoons; too complicated. Even the sailmaker has an electric-powered sewing machine that helped him get through the tough canvas work of putting a riding sail on *Florence*, the little wooden Stonington dragger that is one of the newer additions to the fleet.

There is still plenty of stuff in the attic. One of the most authentic is a model of a fictional boat, Ratty's 14-foot Thames scull. My old friend Lois Darling spent the last few months of her life perfecting it right down to the detail of the luncheon basket with leather strap. She made the perfect little shallop in the traditional dollhouse scale of an inch to the foot, but crewed it with people-sized miniatures of the Rat in proper river garb of the Edwardian era and the Mole in his landsman's waistcoat but with his tie off and his collar open for the warm spring day. The boat was for a time in the Children's Museum in a nicely accessible location, but later it was put away and the curators haven't found a permanent place for it. I hope they will. So many yachtsmen and women learned first of the delights of messing about in boats from that lovely little craft in *The Wind in the Willows* that it seems a pity not to have the model of the real thing out where it can be seen.

Mystic Seaport is least well enjoyed by the hurried tourist that has to "get through it" before the end of a one or even a two day visit. Just lounging around the place, listening and looking, gives the greatest return. I rounded the green, hearing the chanteyman lead a chorus of visitors in an anchor-lifting ditty with words of several possible levels of meaning. The *Morgan* was dressed in topsails, fore course, and a couple of jibs. As I stood on the Chubb wharf beside her, the afternoon southwester made her heel gently toward the dock and the gang plank slid a foot or more back and forth on a sheet-iron landing plate. It was nice to hear her creak with the motion. Years ago, when I first came to Mystic, she was bedded down in the mud of the river bottom, held there by her ballast in all but the highest spring tides, but she has been afloat again now for fifteen or twenty years and her bottom planking is still the same century and a half old oak that she was built with. Out beyond her, two dozen little Dyers were tacking about in a confusion of primary colored sails. Every so often they would fall into a regular pattern quite magically as the inaudible starting horn for the next race brought them all onto the same tack at the same instant. The livery catboat *Breck Marshall* passed inside them on the way up the river with a half dozen passengers aboard. Her big gaff-headed mainsail had a patch of new material in it. The two tones of sail cloth added to her authenticity. She is a perfectly beautiful boat in any case, but one that gains grace from age even though she is a reproduction, built only a few years ago in the Seaport's own Boatshop.

Back in *Blueberry*'s cabin I listened to the NOAA weather forecast and consulted *Eldridge's Tide and Pilot Book* for the details of my return voyage on the following day. The flood was scheduled to turn fair at the Race between Fisher's Island and Plum Island by 0800. That would give me until half past two in the afternoon to be inside the estuary of the Connecticut if I was to have a ride on the tide in Long Island Sound and a lift up the river to home. *Blueberry*'s engine can handle the current of the river well enough, but the wind was to be the predictable southwest summer zephyr, perhaps strengthening to 15 to 20 in the afternoon, and I would have to tack against it. Beating to windward across a falling tide of two and a half knots would reduce my speed over the bottom to something like a knot and a half or two even in a good wind, with *Blueberry* doing her best hull speed of around five and a half to six. At that pace I would spend all day and some of the night on the trip home. The tide is always more important than the wind for a small sailboat in Long Island Sound. The last time I had tried such a course, the wind freshened to more then twenty and the rising tide was pushed into quite a fearful chop on the seaward side of all the points projecting from the Connecticut shore. Either more wind or less, an early start to the west was obviously a good idea.

But even the 0715 bridge opening at Mystic would leave me with several hours of sailing before I got past Sea Flower reef and out into the Sound where the rising tide could benefit me. I decided to get down the Mystic River and out past Mason's Island before the early dark of September required my anchoring for the night. The chart revealed a bight on the east side of Ram Island, just east of Noank, that looked like an appropriate harbor, out of the way of the swells pushed up by the prevailing westerly winds. Given the distance and the time of sunset, I decided to push for the five fifteen bridge opening. Given the state of my galley and the prospect of a second tinned dinner in two days, I concluded that a four o'clock supper at the bar of the Seaman's Inne would do nicely.

The Inne's bar is one of the better remodelings of that often altered restaurant. The ceiling is ancient, stamped sheet metal painted cream, the Thonet bentwood chairs have dark red plush seats, and the menu is written on a chalk board just to the left of the door. A solitary diner is accommodated at a high bar stool at any hour of the day. Even if it weren't on the posted list, the pleasant bartender said he could produce a lobster salad and a sidel of Samuel Adams bitter. Since feeding oneself is the least expense of supporting a sailboat, I figured I could order *á la carte* with impunity. Even with a side order of french fries.

We caught the bridge opening at 1715 handily and powered down the Mystic anchorage, following the zigzag of the channel most of the way, but the tide was nearly full and I cut in between boats that seemed to have as much draught as we, making a course more or less directly for the north horn of the crescent of Ram Island. This was a new anchorage for me, but it was attractively described in the *Complete Boating Guide*. I came in from the north-east, being passed along the way by an able looking lobster fisherman power boat with "Ram Island" and "Mystic" lettered on its transom. When I entered the shallow bay it was tied up at the somewhat shaky looking dock on the other horn of the cove.

A wire fence bisects the waist of the island, separating a middling large house with attendant trees and lawns on the left side from scrub vegetation on the other. I assumed that the sheep would be on the right but I saw none. Gulls were plentiful on the right and a single child in a yellow sweater squatted by the waterside on the other side. The water in the little bay was very clear and I could see the individual blades of grass on the bottom eight or nine feet below. I lowered the Bruce, paid out thirty feet of rode and backed down on the diesel to dig it in. Bruce anchors are meant to be good for anything from rock to mud but are not especially recommended for kelp or thick grass. It seemed to take hold quickly however, and I have never dragged since I've had it.

A half dozen adults and another child seemed to surround parts of the house, but the place had a disused aspect and even though windows on both sides of the house allowed me to see right through it, the silhouetted forms didn't appear to be preparing supper or even having cocktails. They gave more of the impression of caretakers than owners of the little island. As the evening settled the whole island took on a blue-grey cast against the pink and ochre sky. The shore line was black and very dark green except for the sweater of the child who seemed to be gathering mussels from the rocks. After a while the grownups came outside and called for the girl in the yellow sweater. There was some bustling back and forth to the dock and around seven o'clock they all boarded the lobster boat and set out towards the mainland at flank speed with navigation lights burning. In all the time I had observed them I don't think anyone ever gave *Blueberry* so much as a passing glance. I guess they were used to having visitors in their anchorage in the summer months.

A number of years ago I had sent a couple of miniature bottles of Bushmill's Irish Whiskey to the mother of a friend who was hospitalized. The friend returned the favor and I still had the little bottles in the spice rack of *Blueberry*'s galley. They seemed appropriate for the wilder end of the uninhabited island. I also had a chunk of Jarlsburg, a nectarine and oatmeal cookies to make a complement to my early supper in Mystic. I sat in the cockpit while an orange sun settled slowly over the rocks of the northwestern end of the island. Then I retired to more Mozart in the cabin. Prescott (which I have been working on for several years) having failed to keep me up to nine on the previous evening, I switched to Procopius' *Secret History* with little more success in spite of some racy stuff about the formative years of the

Empress Theodora. I set the anchor light and turned in.

The little cove supplied a somewhat more agitated berth than I had expected and I couldn't quite tell what was causing the short quick swells, the wind being gentle and coming from the island side of my mooring with only a hundred feet of fetch for the wind to press upon the water. After a tighter lashing of the tiller and securing the tintinabulating traveler of the staysail horse, I slept tolerably well until first light, around 5 AM.

The dawn came up pink and grey behind us with visibility of about a quarter of the mile beyond the opening of the cove. I heard the rhythmic cluck of oars being pulled smartly against oar locks and shortly saw a double scull appear out of the fog to the south and move easily across the opening between the horns of the cove. I waved, but the two oarsmen stuck to their business and disappeared shortly into the surrounding mist, making good time towards Mystic or

Stonington. They appeared to have a good idea of where they were going, but given the visibility or lack of it, I judged that they had a compass fixed to a thwart aft of the stroke oar's feet.

After the departure of the scullers I was quite alone again. Even only a half mile off Mason's Island and in between Fisher's Island and Noank, the east side of Ram Island felt totally removed from the company of other humanity. I loved visiting it, but I can't imagine living in that lonely house without a flock of guests, servants, or children. I don't mind being unsociable on a boat where I can always alter course and sail back to civilization, but the lone house on the island seemed too much of a hermitage for me. Living there must give one the feeling of being extraneous to the whole world. I hauled up the anchor and got underway at 0640.

The sun was red this morning, but it seemed to portend no warning for sailors in any way that I could see. The air had been still at dawn, but within a half hour, a dozen knots of southwest wind came up and I was just able to fetch sea room around Noank on the port tack. Groton Long Point loomed ahead. I tacked to the south and passed a lobsterman hauling his pot and skillfully extracting its contents. I gave him good morning and asked if he were doing well with his catch.

"Lot of shawts this mawnin," he observed, tossing an adolescent lobster back into the sea.

The down east accent of the state of Maine has a tendency to extend south on the coast all the way to Boston and then continues off shore to Long Island. I sometimes think you might still hear it in New Jersey if you stayed a couple of miles out to sea. Anyway, Stonington, Connecticut, sounds like Stonington, Maine, when you meet the people on the water.

Two more tacks took me in close to Mumford Cove and around the Horseshoe Reef buoy and back out towards

Seaflower. I managed to weather Little Dumpling, tacked close to the shore of Fisher's Island and took a reasonably long board toward New London, leaving the brick Victorian house of the harbor light on my starboard hand. Trying to stretch the tack to the west to get beyond reach of the tide that was starting to make up the Thames, I put the engine on for a little lift to windward. To my surprise, the reliable little Vetus slowed down and stopped altogether in a few minutes. This had happened in prior years and was a sign of air in the fuel line. Restarting in a few minutes seemed to work it out. The system is supposed to be "self bleeding," but the experience didn't give me much of a feeling of confidence about the possibility of tide rips off the Connecticut shore points along the way home. Best to stay off shore if the countervailing wind and tide began to push up a chop.

By 0940 I passed Sarah Ledge and was tacking south towards The Race, ignoring the beginnings of the flood until I was able to get well beyond Race Rock where Captain George Eldridge's little current charts told me to expect better than two and a half under my transom, boosting me off to the west. The wind was dropping and presently it seemed that I was going nowhere at all, even though the sails were full and seemed to be drawing. There was a greasy wake of slack water to starboard, but the bubbles stood still beside me. I pushed the "go" button on the diesel and gathered way. There was a funny lurch to the helm and a muffled bump from under the keel. Looking aft I found two large lobster pot buoys bobbing to the surface behind me. I don't know what the fisherman used as an anchor for his pot, but it was evidently quite enough to hold *Blueberry* fast when I had fouled his warp.

By 1150 I was well beyond where the square lone skeletal tower that marks Bartlett's Reef rises out of the ruffled surface of the sea. The tides make odd patterns where they pass the seaward end of Bartlett's and the dimpled and prickly look of the water has always given me a feeling of apprehension. Even though the sounder showed better than twenty five feet beneath me, I couldn't help feeling that there was something unseen down there that I might find with my keel. I found a blueberry yoghurt in the bottom of the cooler where even the ice was lasting well. It made a delicious elevensies.

My next southern tack was nearly due south, across the grain of the tide, but the longitude displayed on the loran continued to tick off another hundredth of a minute of westing every minute or so; the tide was pushing me toward home even as I sailed the short board of the starboard tack to get my course free of Black Point to fetch the Connecticut River. The little Loran is an amazing gadget; it keeps telling me where I am within a range of about sixty feet. Every time I pass a buoy or prick it off on the chart, it seems wonderfully close to the mark.

I had added the Loran to the ship's equipment after an experience in these same waters two years earlier. I was south of Black Point in a gentle afternoon breeze when a great grey fog came drifting in from the sound and shut down visibility to less than thirty yards just as I entered Niantic Bay. I set a compass course for the entrance to the Niantic River and went in with care, watching the depth sounder. That bottom is rather flat and featureless, but presently I heard a sort of mezzo soprano chain saw whine and a red and black plastic Jet-ski came whizzing out of the murk and crossed my bow. The rider reigned in his machine and circled back towards me.

"Mister," he shouted, "You're heading for the rocks!"

I thanked him and asked where away the entrance of the Niantic River.

"Over there," he said, pointing into the grey off my starboard bow.

By my reckoning the indicated course would have put me on the shore by the Millstone power plant, but I am a great respecter of what navigators call "local knowledge" and I had turned in the direction he indicated. In five minutes the red and green markers of the river channel came marching towards me out of the fog. The experience made me far more tolerant of Jet-skis, even if they are noisy, too fast, and don't look like boats. It also convinced me that now that Loran was available and cheap, it was high time to buy one.

When one is working one's way up the Sound on a fair tide, there is, in me at least, a tendency to stay too far to the north side in the belief that it gets the boat closer to her eventual destination. But the power of the tide is well out in the center, three or four miles from the Connecticut shore or even more. In spite of my best resolution, I found myself short changing my southerly tacks and starting too soon to the west again. It is hard to keep moving the ship away from her destination just to get into position to make a better shot at the goal later on.

By 1300 the wind died and I switched over to power. With both tide and diesel pushing me towards Saybrook light I was making better than six knots over the bottom according to the C/S display on the Loran. I cut inside the eastern breakwater and passed the inner light on Saybrook Point by half past two. Once in the River, a nice southwest onshore breeze came up and then tended into the west. I killed the Vetus which had been behaving erratically and broke out the rest of the Jarlsburg, crackers and the penultimate nectarine for lunch. Cheese, crackers and fruit are the ideal lunch while under sail. They don't slip around like the innards of a sandwich and they require no plate. The whole collation can be dumped in a bowl with a nonskid bottom without getting the ingredients mixed up. A pocket knife serves to slice the cheese and section the fruit. I chipped off a chunk of the dwindling ice and filled a plastic double old fashioned glass with lime-flavored seltzer and a tot of Mount Gay Rum. The boat sails herself very well in the River and the railroad bridge stayed open just long enough for me to get through. I ran easily before the wind past Essex by three o'clock. North of Ely's Ferry a trio of little white herons decorated the rocks. The osprey was on duty and the top of Daymarker #29. I took in the jib and staysail at the mouth of Hamburg Cove by 1520. Inside I powered up toward Al Hine's dock while furling the main and flemishing down the jib sheets and backstay pennants. Al's dock is decorated by a flag and Lee's box of pretty red geraniums, but there was no boat there; *Sunshine* was sold late that summer and her replacement, somewhat smaller, may not be secured until next year.

At 1550 I tied up at Bennet's Dock, whence I started two

and a half days earlier. Ten hours of working mostly to windward is a long day, but not at all unpleasant. I gathered up my sail bag of clothing and dry stores in one hand and took the cooler in the other, snapped the lock on the cabin hatch, and walked off to the pickup truck in the yacht club parking lot.

II. *Before Blueberry*

My first boat was a donated Penguin Dinghy with a hole in the bow and a shattered centerboard. Repaired, painted seaweed green, and her perforated sail patched with scraps of bright red awning cloth, she was lovely in the eye of the beholders. The greatest adventure of sailing her was getting out of the Inner Cove at Hamburg and into the Outer Cove. Reaching the River itself was a project for an all-day excursion with picnic lunch. My greatest day's journey was with my younger daughter, Amity, aged five years and wrapped in a bulging orange PFD. Wedged between the mast and the centerboard trunk, she chattered happily about everything under the sun while I sailed the boat, grimly and with purpose, through the shifting tides into the river and up the shore past Joshua Rock to a little sandy beach on the east shore just short of the westerly turn past Brockway Ferry. We beached the little boat and I undid all four of our sneakers to go ashore for lunch before heading back down the river. The whole day's voyage was about three and a half miles on the rhumb line and required close to five hours to complete.

The boat never really had a name, although "Seaweed" was nominated. Mostly she was referred to as "the Penguin." I sold her for $25 to a Nursery School teacher who had once been a nun. She developed a taste for sailing and shipped out to the Azores with a man she met in a boat yard in New Jersey. She moved to Hawaii and I lost contact with her. Before she went, she sold the Penguin to another teacher who, being of German surname, christened her *Deutschland* and painted her hull a raffish black. After that I lost track.

Eventually she was succeeded by a Jacque Heubelot plywood sloop of a certain age, eighteen feet overall, and French in appearance with a reverse sheer to her deck. We named her *Tinúviel* for the elvish maid that danced under the hemlock umbels in J.R.R.Tolkien's *Lord of the Rings*. There were lots of hemlocks along the shores of Hamburg Cove in those days. Our children were then growing like olive shoots about our board and in the recesses of our home. We had six by then, all of them still under twelve.

Tinúviel had a pair of quarter berths and a sort of padded V-space in the forepeak. She had auxiliary power in the shape of an elderly British Seagull. I managed to drop the original into Hamburg Cove and had to replace it with one of even lower power that lacked a clutch. Once when she was brand new to us, we loaded the whole eight members of the family aboard in the late summer evening, lighted the running lights and circumnavigated Brockway Island in the Connecticut River by night. We sailed her all over the place: Long Island Sound, Gardiners Bay, to New London for the Yale-Harvard regatta, up the Niantic River, to Mattituck, Fisher's Island and Mystic, but mostly in the lovely lower Connecticut River. Once using the boat hook to sound the depth, I took her up the creek through Selden's Cove and out through the rushes into the River again.

Innocent of current charts of Long Island sound, a dear friend and I once undertook an evening sail from New London to Hamburg Cove against a falling tide. Little Gull light, the unblinking white one, hung motionless over our left shoulder for what must have been four hours. Eventually we came upon a large unlighted object floating in the placid and nearly windless Sound. The swirl of tide around it just about matched our speed in the opposite direction. With a flashlight we made it out to be a buoy labled with a cryptic "HP." We had no idea what it indicated and found no sign of it on the small craft chart we were using. Buoys seem huge when you are close to them in a small boat and this one loomed over our heads as we crept past it. We ignited the Seagull and pressed on for home. We reached Hamburg Cove after four in the morning. My friend's wife had not slept and spent the waking hours planning our memorial service since obviously the bodies would never be recovered from the sea. My wife slept peacefully, knowing that I would always be late getting home from a sail.

Tinúviel was a nifty little overnighter with a Seaswing stove and room for an ample ice chest. Christopher, our oldest, and I took her to Mystic. Adam and Charity, second son and first daughter, went to Sag Harbor and came back in a breeze of wind that scared the daylights out of father and mother but left the two young happily unfazed by the white caps that broke from the top of the six-foot chop that we beat into all the way from Plum Gut to Saybrook. Later we learned how to reef the mainsail. Ben, the third son, accompanied me on a three-day jaunt to Fisher's Island and back up the Sound to Clinton in a squall of rain followed by a lobster dinner. Finally, I sold the little sloop in a period of financial discouragement while my youngest son, Noah, was away at camp. He felt he had been ill-used, cheated behind his back while he was garnering camp honors as a sailor. We mollified him by taking him along as crew when we chartered boats in several successive summers. We cruised to Newport and Vineyard Haven, to Cutty Hunk and Block Island, but the Principle of Dissatisfaction continued to assert itself: those lovely chartered and borrowed vessels were not *our* boat and none of them was perfect even in its own terms.

It is said that the desire to build a boat begins as a small cloud, hardly visible on the horizon of consciousness. It grows unseen, while one's back is turned, until almost without warning it covers the sky from east to west and blots out the distant view of almost everything else. A Portuguese proverb: for a man to have lived he has to have planted a tree, raised a son and built a boat. My four sons were far from done with growing up inside or outside of my attempts at guiding them. Arboreal cultivation, thinning, pruning, transplanting and even spraying, were all about me in the little property that we had bought on a venture of extended debt in Connecticut. Such a man also requires a patient and forgiving wife.

How does one begin to build a boat? Lacking prior experience save for the repair of the Penguin, I turned to a "frame set"; not quite a kit boat, but far easier than starting from scratch with a set of plans and a lumber list. Clark Craft of Tonnawanda, New York, then as now had an intriguing catalogue of designs that could be provided with pre-cut frames. Set up on a "strong back" of 2 x 6 timbers, these could be planked with quarter inch marine plywood to make a hull that would be virtually sure to have accurately fair curves if the frames were positioned accurately. Lofting, that is drawing out the plans in full size on the floor, would not be necessary since the dimensions of the sawn frames were presumably accurate when they came out of the box from Tonnawanda.

But the snub-nosed little sloop, technically known as a "Hartley Trailer-Sailor Twelve" for her length and her naval architect, seemed to us to lack something of traditional saltiness and perhaps of the sail area needed for the light summer winds of the Connecticut River. While the hull was under construction in the barn on the weekends and academic vacations over that winter and spring, back in New York where I served as Headmaster of Saint David's School, I began drawing changed sail plans. The result was a gaff rig for the main, one that reminded me of the cat boats I learned to sail in. To balance all that sail out back, I added a three foot bowsprit to support a club-footed jib. The resulting profile lost all resemblance to the original, especially with the addition of a "cat's eye" oval port light to the side of the little cuddy. Lois Darling later suggested curving the line that joined the cockpit coaming to the trunk of the cuddy and when all was done the result looked not unlike a miniature Friendship Sloop, or one seen at a great distance in conditions of reduced visibility.

All of my sons and daughters got involved with the project in one way or another. At Christmas an enormous package standing clear of the Christmas tree was in due season delivered of a British Seagull outboard motor that stood gleaming in the New York City living room for several weeks.

The boat went together with surprising ease. Noah and I put a lot of bronze ring nails into the mahogany and lined the contact surfaces between the plywood and the "hondo" (as the lumber yard men called it) with neatly torn strips of old bed sheeting stuck down in bedding compound. This was, according to the book, supposed to make her "tight as a cup." It did, but we later found out about the Gougeon Brothers W.E.S.T. system and used epoxy ever after.

We settled on *Tom Bombadil* for a name, honoring another Tolkien character. This one was a fine fellow who followed the River's Daughter and whose magic was quite strong if he didn't get too far away from home, less so thereafter. His song suggested the color scheme.

> Ho, Tom Bombadil!
> He's a merry fellow.
> Bright blue his jacket is,
> And his boots are yellow...

We painted the topsides a very strong blue and added a yellow boot top stripe. Decks were standard New England fisherman's buff and the cuddy and coaming sides were the traditional white. A pair of decorated boards on either side of the stem were lettered in large Bembo caps with the name, and when she went into the water at Mystic (a romantic gesture in honor of other, older wooden boats), the derivation of her title was immediately recognized with approving shouts by the crew of strong young collegians pulling the oars of one of the Seaport's whale boats.

The maiden voyage back from Mystic with failing winds and a faltering outboard was undertaken by Noah and Charity as far as the Mile Creek beach, in Lyme, east of the mouth of the Connecticut River. For the last few miles he sat astride the bow and paddled while his sister kept the course. Admiration and drinks and sunburn unguent were served around to all. Later I took her back to Saybrook with friend Steve Diamond. We brought along some ice and the Mount Gay Rum Collinses from the beach gathering, but we both neglected to wear our glasses and neither of us could read the soundings on the chart that I had carefully provided. Boiling along to windward in the afternoon southwester, well heeled over, we put her hard on the bar off Griswold Point and managed to crack the dagger board. But nothing broken on a home-built boat stays unfixed for long and I took the board home in the car to repair overnight.

Two days later, my wife Cathy and I set out by airplane on a family visit to Oregon, leaving Noah, just turned seventeen, in charge of the boat. He had at that time a fancy for a girl that lived in Westport, some seventy nautical miles farther up the sound. He packed the ice chest with cheese, crackers, V-8 and Pop-tarts, stowed foul weather gear and a tarpaulin and set off. It took three days to get to Westport, but the boat was admired in each anchorage and he was invited for drinks he was too young to be allowed by the skippers who were curious about the little vessel. He modestly admitted to having built her, a truthful claim, as he had surely as much to do with her construction as I. When he reached his destination he was able to say to the young lady:

I wanted to come see you, so I built this boat and...

On the way back the weather promised to turn foul, so he telephoned his sister and got the trailer brought as far as Black Rock to pick him up. They headed home shortly before the storm.

Finding a proper place to moor *Tom Bombadil* in the Outer Cove led to the building of our first Phil Bolger boat, the 10'6" "Pointy Skiff," an instant boat done from plans provided by Dynamite Payson of South Thomaston, Maine. Although lofting wasn't required for this tender, it was not a kit of prepared materials and the fact that it went together in six mornings during a school spring vacation made Noah and me feel like proper shipwrights. We painted it bright red but added a yellow boot top to keep in some relationship with the mother ship. The Seagull powered her with authority and, being high sided and broad bottomed, the boat proved to be both rugged and seaworthy although she was light enough for one man to haul out and slide into the back of a pick-up truck, one end at a time.

I painted the name *Gimli*, one of Tolkien's more benevolent dwarfs, on her transom, but somehow it never stuck and repainting the name every season got to be a chore. Everybody referred to it as "the red rowboat." She was constructed of 9 mm. plywood of questionable durability and depended greatly on the epoxy sealer to stave off delamination. Her greatest virtue was eternal readiness and portability.

Once we gave room and board to a young German law student doing an internship at the United Nations for the greater part of a spring semester. His name was Christophe and his English was good when he came, excellent by the time he left. During our late March spring break, I took him up to the Connecticut house for a long weekend to show him something of America other than New York City. On a sunny and breezy March day we shoved the red boat into the back of the pickup, took oars, motor, a box of crackers, a bottle of tawny port and my ancient and long deceased father-in-law's set of little silver cups in their leather traveling case. We put the boat in behind the causeway on the Cove Road in Hamburg and ran under the bridge and then up past the marina and Reynolds' boatyard. The tide was full and we were able to go up the Eight Mile River to the three arches of the Joshuatown Road bridge and beyond. Although the river bank lacks the pollard trees, the bridge is reminiscent of Ernest Shepard's drawings in *The Wind in the Willows*.

There was a little bit of warmth in the late March sunshine and the breeze was just bearable on the water. We went down the length of the Cove at a good clip and headed out into the River. The south end of Brockway Island is a little sandy beach, about twenty feet long at high tide. We pulled the boat up on the sand and ate cheese and crackers with a splash of port in the little silver cups.

I explained to Christophe that although the Connecticut was unadorned by the commercial traffic of the Rhine, it too had castles along its banks, there being two just up river from where we were: William Gillette's extraordinary lair at Hadlyme and the brooding, turreted presence of Saint John's, a school for boys in need of supervision on the western shore in Deep River.

The river was devoid of other boats, recreational or

commercial. The banks were pale brown and yellow but there was some green showing at the water line of the marsh grasses on either side of the entrance to the Cove. The osprey hadn't yet made their comeback from the DDT era

at that date in the early seventies and there were no cormorants in the river in March, but we saw a pair of swans that had apparently wintered over in the lower valley. We started up the Seagull, powered back to our starting point, hauled the boat to the truck and put it back in the barn to await the summer season.

Tom Bombadil had many virtues, principal among which was a certain cuteness that aroused a lot of favorable comment, but she had inherent vices too. The gaff-rig and increased sail area gave her a strong weather helm which the small jib did little to overcome. All that top-hamper set on the narrow foredeck made her somewhat unstable if the crew's weight was too far forward. I once came up to the stern of a pair of schooners tied up at the Steamboat Dock in Essex at the close of a traditional vessels regatta shortly after Labor Day. I luffed up smartly under the counter of one and called to a young lady sitting on the taffrail, asking her to hold my headstay. She complied and I busied myself with handing

the sails. She evidently misunderstood the need to hang on
until I had a line across, because she then let go of the stay to
pick up her cocktail glass and I found myself drifting back-
ward on the tide with my sails down in lumps all around me.
Forgetful of balance, I grabbed at the rail of the other
schooner as it went by, put my weight on my foredeck and
slid off over the bow as *Tom Bombadil*'s stern rose in the air
and her mast swung gracefully down to port. The boat
righted itself as soon as it was rid of my offending and off-
balancing weight; a member of one schooner's crew grabbed
a shroud and one from each boat reached down into the
space between them to seize my arms and haul me up to deck
level. Aside from the wet and a couple of sore shoulder
sockets, all was well. I even had a sail bag of dry clothes on
board and so was ready to join the cocktail party.

Late that night, after Stuart Ingersol's banjo and tuba
outdoor chamber quartette had played themselves to ex-
haustion and the revelers had left the dock at the Connecticut River Museum, I spread the boom tent over the cockpit
of *Tom Bombadil* and rolled myself in a comforter for the
night. Sleeping on the water, when it's calm enough, is
always pleasant. In the morning I lit the little Sterno stove in
the boxed "Swedish galley" I kept in the cuddy and made
coffee. Poking my head out of a corner of the unbuttoned
boom tent, still wrapped up in the quilt, I watched a near
perfect sunrise over Nott Island across from the Essex
waterfront. Even a short cruise can take you far away from
home.

But as winter succeeded each summer and I reviewed the
past season, it became more and more clear that the little
gaffer was not our ultimate boat. Overnighting aboard *Tom
Bombadil* was splendid and the Ensolite pad under the quilt
was passingly comfortable, but it wasn't a really weather-
proof cabin with real bunks, and the ship lacked running

lights, a radio, or a library of musical tapes. Most of all, its range was limited and its survival in a serious squall might have been too soon dependent upon the flotation material we had built into her hull. A slightly bigger vessel seemed to be called for. At least one on which you could walk around the outer edge of the deck without suffering a capsize.

Even more to the point, the experiment with the retrofitted gaff rig had given me a fascination with such arcane concepts as Center of Effort and Center of Lateral Plane. I read Howard Chapelle's venerable classic on yacht design, one of a few books still in print that acknowledges the existence of the gaff rig. And a gaffer she should be, if only because of the ease of thus spreading enough sail before the wind to obviate the use of a spinnaker. Large headsails require large crews and a spinnaker needs at least two on board and is better done with three. Single handers like Chichester were able to get them up and down alone, but I am not of that ilk nor ever would be. A Friendship or a Noank Sloop would be a good model to start from, or perhaps one of the small early canoe yawls. Thomas Flemming Day's *Seabird*, Harry Pidgeon's *Islander*, and of course that most famous of singlehanders, Joshua Slocum's *Spray* had all been gaff rigged and did not depend on their headsails for power with the wind abaft the beam. These boats were all yawls, but little sloops like Thomas Gilmer's *Blue Moon* and Sam Rabl's *Piccaroon* were closer to what I thought I could encompass. William Garden, William Atkin, and even the contemporary Bruce Bingham had designed small, gaff headed sloops that worked their way into my subconscious.

The New York living room housed an ancient and truly dysfunctional grand piano of magnificent size. It would not stay in tune for three days and the action was deep and spongy. The hull, however was a lovely old walnut thing that had been rescued from a church basement and stripped of its scarred original finish. Even long after it was no longer playable, it decorated the east end of the room and provided a buffet for the faculty parties. It also kept water color paints and various delicate projects out of the reach of small children. I topped it with a drawing board and set myself to designing in earnest.

The first attempt was 23 feet long and, as worked out by a friend with some skill in naval architecture, would have had a displacement of over 5000 pounds. I tried again and ended up with a hard-chined hull of 19'6" overall with a four foot bowsprit supporting a gaff rig of something like 250 square feet including a small forestaysail. I managed to get an accommodation for two into this envelope, but not one with much privacy for the head. But just imagining being in the cabin was an experience of being warm and dry in foul weather.

I drew and redrew, fiddling with the profile of the cabin trunk, the head room necessary to put on trousers while sort of standing up, and the location of under deck lockers amidships that would move the back of a settee far enough inboard to keep one from perpetually bending the neck forward or else cracking one's head on the edge of the cabin trunk. Room for a good galley and copious tool storage, book shelves, chart stowage, a wine cellar and a proper bulkhead for mounting brass instruments as well as a medium fidelity music system were all worked in. After a full winter of revision I was ready to think about building a boat. On the assumption that construction of a boat of twice the length would cost eight times as much money and take eight times as long to complete, I tried to translate this cube rule into the difference between *Tom Bombadil*'s twelve feet LOA and this new boat's twenty feet. I came out with a building schedule of something approaching seven years and seven quarantines, but I was sure it couldn't take that long.

But even with such a daunting program stretching out into the future, I wasn't yet ready to build it. I couldn't think of committing the material, money and time to my own plan without a very thorough going over by a professional. Perhaps even a total redrawing and refiguring of the whole project would be best. I had studied plans by many of the great designers, but most of them were, being dead, unavailable for consultation. Most of the younger generation had never thought much about the gaff rig. The long career and varied designs of Philip C. Bolger of Gloucester seemed far and away best suited to the project. I had no idea what he might charge or whether he would be willing to take up a design that he had not initiated himself. The idea of commissioning the services of a naval architect seemed altogether too grand for my purse.

But I decided to write him a letter anyway...

III. *Correspondence*

Dear Mr. Bolger,

I have built two boats, one of your 10'6" skiffs and one Hartley 12' which I redesigned as a gaff sloop with a three foot bowsprit. Both boats came out fair and pretty and have given much pleasure. I would like to do an overnighter or coastal singlehander for my mature years (now 54), but I have to get it built before I lack the muscle to bend the plywood.

I have looked at a lot of designs (including most of yours) and, although I admire all, none seems quite what I want. I have essayed a design of my own and have produced some drawings of a sort of latter day Noank sloop that is 19' 6" on deck, perhaps some 23' O.A. with a beam of 7'6" or less and a draft at the deadwood of 2'7"—about right for the Connecticut River area where I have a house and a small barn where I have done my ship building.

The boat I have drawn has a waterline of 16'9" and is hard chined for plywood construction. I fiddled around with the various determinant diagonals from chine to keel face and ended up with a fairly sharp entry and a nearly flat deadrise at the transom, but I have no confidence in my ability to draw it so that I have no compound curves in the plywood. That's where you come in. What does it cost to have the services of your self (or perhaps another N.A. you might recommend) to design a boat that I have sketched out? That is, assuming that you would be willing to design one that looked like the vessel I have drawn—or at least one with the same flavor and accommodation.

I don't have access to a blue printer and the Xerox I have used distorts the drawings one way or another so the scale may be off—they do give the idea though.

Besides lines, I would need a certain number of construction details and would really like projections of the big hull panels, although I suppose I could do this myself from your lines.

Finally, I guess this sort of hull is not susceptible to your exterior chine-log method as in the instant boats. I wish it were. I will use WEST for adhesive and sealer as I did on the skiff and probably make my own spars from laminates of 5/4 fir stair tread. I like mast hoops. Power would be a 6 to 8 horsepower inboard, diesel if I can afford it, or a slow turning one lunger if I can find one.

Then, the question: How much for a set of plans?

Sincerely,
David D. Hume

P.S. I can't draw figures to scale; those on the plan are, with due apology, tracings from an appropriately sized print of Manet's "Dejeuner sur l'herbe" as you may recognize.

Bolger, I later learned, lives on one of his own boats, drafting board and all. Since he has no telephone and has very little extra room in which to leave things lying around, he tends to be a prompt correspondent. His return letter arrived the day after Christmas. The letterhead and the envelope were decorated with a chaste file of silhouettes of large and small yachts and workboats.

Gloucester, December 23, 1981

David D. Hume

Thanks for yours of Decmebr [sic] 16. That would be a very pretty little boat, and I don't think myself you'd come to much grief doing your own designing.

If I was doing it, I think I'd step the mast a few inches farther aft to get more head angle or boom clearance for the staysail...I have my doubts about the water breaker, if only because I wouldn't know where to look for a cooper these days.

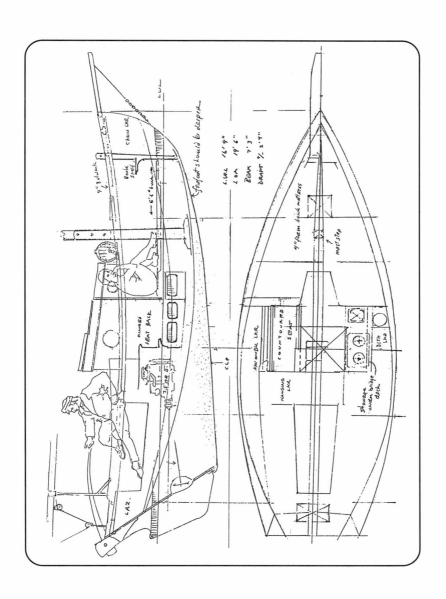

L.W.L. 16' 9"
L.O.A. 19' 6"
BEAM 7' 3"
DRAFT ½ 2' 7"

The hull would sail all right as designed, but I think she'd trim by the stern with anybody in the cockpit, which is the weak point of cruisers as short as this anyway, and is exaggerated by the method of projection used. I'd do as in my CRYSTAL and WOLFTRAP etc, designs with a length of straight rabbet amidships and much more deadrise at the stern. I doubt that prefabricated panels are practical in a shape as complex as this one, though a projection for the topsides might save some trouble getting a good sheer line...

It could be that a little more salient keel forward would be an improvement.

That's about it in the way of comments, except for the usual reminder that she'd be better if she was longer. If you want me to make a set of plans from this study, I'll do it for $750[1]. That strikes me as being too high a proportion of the cost of the boat, and incidentally it won't be done very quickly as I have about a three-month backlog of work at the moment. If you'd like me to just lay off a set of hull lines, I'll do that for $200 and probably quicker, but that doesn't include any advice on the rest of it.

Phil. C. Bolger

I wouldn't "come to much grief doing your own designing." What a hearty New England compliment lurked in that laconic phrase! I leapt to the drawing board to add a foot to the waterline of the little vessel, to add "salient keel" forward, and to get more buoyancy under the stern. I sent the resulting sketch back in early January.

---

[1]Translating the money of the early eighties into today's values is a little like determining the worth of the Roman denarius or the penny of Chaucerian England. Asking P.C.B. what he would charge for *Blueberry* today might produce a ratio that would be of interest to the Harvard Business School or even the post-privatization theorists of the former Soviet Union.

Dear Philip Bolger,

Your letter encouraged me greatly and I have taken your comments to heart...resketching the profile. I have added about a foot to the waterline and nine inches to the deck in the hope of creating a little more buoyancy aft and have also given the run a considerable deadrise. I have not, however attempted to project that twisty plywood bottom strake, so that I really don't know if the profile along the rabbet has anything to do with reality or not. I have provided more salient keel forward, scrapped the breaker, and stepped the mast a half a foot farther aft....

The sketch enclosed changes the dimensions to give a little more width of trunk so that the settee doesn't leave you banging your neck on the side of the cabin. There is also a little less beam to the hull and the engine has been shifted aft three or four inches to make the settee accommodate two in a pinch.

Questions: Is any kind of MSD available that would fit under the bunk where I have given it such small clearance?

Would there be any advantage in setting the engine on the diagonal to make for simpler and stronger work on the deadwood; although I guess I should bite the bullet and learn how to do it the right way with a three foot auger.

I realize I have paid an inordinate amount of attention to the accommodation, but the real design job after all is yours and I want to be sure that in a hull so small we have left the requisite few inches here and there that can make all the difference in comfort to man and wife on occasional over-nights.

I am enclosing a check for half of the design fee because I have it handy right now and it might make you feel guilty enough to get me the requisite lines for lofting so that I can start the task and perhaps get the frames cut out before the end of the academic year. While I am still in New York I have a small gymnasium available as a loft floor. Press on whenever you have the time to take it up. I am very excited about the project and look forward to the next three years or so of work on it.

Sincerely yours,
David D. Hume

Bolger's answer arrived promptly, six days later.

January 13, 1982

David D. Hume

Thanks for the check. I'll get on with it as soon as I can, but there are a couple of things I'm already disgracefully behind on, that I <u>must</u> catch up. It'll be at least six weeks and more likely two months before I can hand you much detail: I'll try to give you some lofting offsets before that.

Offhand I see no reason to make any appreciable changes in your design. I like the sheer and profile very much, subject to checking the three-dee effect of the sheer/plan view combination. I may want to alter the deck plan slightly after that.

I've been having very good luck with off-center propellers set close to the centerline and with a faired recess in the deadwood to give tip clearance. Several boats arranged this way handled just like centerline props under power while seeming to benefit appreciably under sail. However, in a boat as light as this one, I'd be reluctant to use a solid prop set out in the open. Were you planning to pay for and accept the rather poor thrust of a folding propeller? Unless I hear from you to the contrary, I'll assume the folding prop and design for off-center...

One change from your study I would like to make would be to bring the sternpost up outside the transom, thereby strengthening the keel against side impacts, and avoiding a messy cut through the keel apron, and also reducing the rake of the rudder post slightly which I think will benefit handling.

There may be room for a Portapotti under the berth... [but] I don't like this location myself and have been advocating stowing the toilet under a hatch in the stern where it can be used under a small tent at anchor, and whence it can be used elsewhere under sail.

Peter Duff (Edey and Duff) looked at your design and liked it....

Phil. Bolger

I left him alone for a couple of weeks, but I couldn't resist fiddling with my own drawings and the ideas that he brought up. I did stop sending him my own sketches at this point and contented myself by cutting out a set of thin wooden sections, mounting them across a cutout profile of the keel, and planking them with colored bristol board. The resulting model was a fair representation of the hull as originally drawn. I turned tiny taffrail stanchions on Ben Hume's little Dremel lathe, but the rail looked pretentious and I scrapped the idea. I also researched lofting materials through architect friend Sam White who discovered that I could get mylar drafting film, 3 ml thick and 54" wide. Two lengths taped together would fit the whole project.

I wrote back to Bolger in early February.

Dear Phil Bolger,

Thanks for your last letter and the encouraging comments from you and Peter Duff. I know little about folding propellers except that even a small one goes for about $250. I think I could put up with that but I worry more about poor thrust. With a 7 h.p. diesel we ought to have plenty of power for this boat but I would hate to be pushing through the rip at Plum Gut and find that the prop just can't quite master the 4.5 kt. tide. Other than that kind of eventuality I would be happy with the off-center configuration. Would [that]...make it possible to have a locker opposite [the engine] where a portable head could be stowed? My wife agrees with your distaste for the location I originally drew.

I agree on sternpost outside — although the extreme rake

of the transom itself is somewhat important to the design.

I lack a profile of the BMW 7 h.p. but do have one of the Faryman which I enclose. We should allow enough space for either (or perhaps the Volvo 7 h.p.) since I must do more research on them. I would love to shorten the portion of the bridge deck inside the cabin— or at least lower it to the counter height if we don't need all the space for the engine.

But I must stop kibitzing. Please follow your own principles, upon which I can rely. I asked you to do it in the first place because I admire your work and don't wish to make life difficult for you.

Sincerely yours,
David D. Hume

Bolger's response revealed that he had been drawing and measuring as well as thinking about the project. The oversized envelope contained a blueprint of the accommodation, a profile and a set of carefully sketched cross sections of the hull.

February 6, 1982

David D. Hume

I had a preliminary look at your project yesterday, and I'm in difficulties; to wit, there is not room in the bow for the berths as proposed. To get the 13" breadth at the end marked on your drawing, they have to be moved aft at least 6", which fouls up the arrangement abaft the berths. They can't be raised and still have the sitting and roll-over height needed. The best idea I've had so far is shown on the enclosed hasty tracing. The sink would be replaced with a bucket or basin placed on the sole between the berths. The cabin heater I was going to argue against in any case on the grounds that one lit kerosene lamp would be enough to heat a cabin of as small volume as this.

Reflecting on your comments I've reverted to the on-center prop, solid two-blade, with enough deadwood behind it to keep it from spoiling the rudder action. Any probable engine should fit without difficulty, even something like the Westerbeke 13, for instance.

I've shown the transom reduced in rake and wider at the chine than you indicate. It can be put back the way you had it if you feel strongly enough about the aesthetics, but the great problem of all designs of this size and type is getting enough bearing aft to carry the crew weight without dragging the tail, so give me all you can stand. She'd behave appreciably better with a vertical transom....

The toilet location indicated seems to me to have everything to be said for it. I seem to have concluded that it could go under the berth by using a 3/4" scale on a 1" drawing. The presence of the gallows should make it very handy to tent over this area....

This bottom is not projected, time not having been taken to do it. The convexity shown is an educated guess as to where it will end up. The chine and rabbet lines are close to what they will have to be if she's to float satisfactorily.

Let me know what you make of this. It'll be some weeks before I can do more on it.

Phil. Bolger

For the first time, a few flickers of disagreement seemed to have appeared. The accompanying drawing showed a berthing compartment shifted aft and a somewhat truncated "saloon" with a single passenger "easy chair" substituted for the little settee. It provided for a little more sleeping space, but at the expense of quite a bit less day cabin. I figured that I would spend more time sitting in the boat than sleeping in it and thus decided to resist this change.

15 February 1982

Dear Phil Bolger,

Thanks for the letter and drawing. I will list a whole series of things that it brings up, with some sense of trepidation about how hard I should push in one area or another. My self-doubt stems from the fact that I so greatly respect your taste, ability and experience that I tend to regard your changes as a sort of Revealed Truth emanating from the Olympian fastness of Gloucester and that they should be carved on wooden, if not stone tablets. I have strong feelings about getting certain things into the design if it is at all possible. Perhaps what I want most of all is to be sure you don't let me insist on anything really stupid while I am trying to cram an overly elaborate accommodation into this little hull. So, here are my reactions:

1. The decreased rake of the transom looks like 3° which is just barely visible to my eye on the plan. Okay by me.

2. If we are really in a jam for LOA I suppose we could throw in another 3" amidships and end up with an even 20'6" LOA....

3. The toes of the berths need not be so wide as 13" each; 9" per side would be plenty, making a total width which would let the berths go back forward where they were. I am 5'11" but my wife is 5'4" and our feet would overlap nicely. Anyone cruising on this size vessel is likely to be in a pretty affectionate relationship surely, and close quarters for the feet would be at least supportable and perhaps pleasant.

4. Likewise, the settee which can thus have a sitting space of 34" would allow two close companions to sit side by side at least occasionally, and also make the lounging space for the singlehander positively luxurious. A day sailing party of four could also seek shelter as I have drawn it.

5. I am glad you ignored the taffrail stanchions. I have built a cardboard plank on frame model of my first design and took the trouble to turn a set of supports for the after rail. They look pretentious on an otherwise clean little ship. I propose we finish off the stern with a bulwark to match the sides, leaving a slot for the tiller. Also thanks for shortening the axe

handle; I note that it now clears the gallows posts.

6. I have raised the sole of the lazarette to match the cockpit and thus allow the potti to be slid farther aft and preserve a ...[larger] footwell so that three could sit to windward if daysailing with a party of four...I very much like the aft location for the head. While underway, ladies can use a chamber pot in the cabin for a simple necessity, reserving the tented potti for more serious business at anchor.

7. The cockpit coaming should be quite a bit higher than I drew it. Something like 10" forward curving down to 8" aft with a sloping filler inside would make a much better support for the back.

8. I put back 6" worth of bridge deck for three reasons: to provide a sheer-height location for a main midships beam for strength; to provide a place to put things handed up from the galley as well as to give a logical location for the compass (too near the engine?), and to make a seven foot side to side shelf in the cabin for books, kitchen gear and other stuff.

9. I notice you put the off-center hatch back amidships.... I was trying to get the standing space over towards the stove, and possibly locating the compass on the after house bulkhead a bit nearer the centerline.

10. I would leave space as drawn for a small sink. I agree that dishes are best done in a bucket, but a 9" round sink would be useful for other purposes.

11. I love the long legged tabernacle that allows the mast to rest on the gallows; great for the Erie Canal or traversing Burgundy.

12. The deadwood change is fine, but how do you draw the shaft if that becomes necessary? A breakaway section of deadwood with bronze plates on its sides for through bolts?

13. I was amazed at the 4000# displacement! It is 1/3 more than I had figured, but that is why you are doing the design work rather than me. It occurs to me that only about 1500# of the weight is in metal (or anything denser than wood) and that this might be supported by 30 cu.ft. of styrofoam blocks

that could be secured in the area between chine and deck outboard of the coaming (still leaving generous lockers under the seats), under the cabin sole, the forward half of the bunks and in the forepeak under the chain locker. Would this give the whole positive buoyancy and thus render the ship virtually unsinkable?

15. The more I hear about the Faryman 7.5 diesel, the better it sounds. It is quite small and might allow a lower engine hatch in the cockpit. It is also a great deal cheaper than the bigger Westerbeke. The mark is some place about $.42 at the moment, but it will probably escalate again before I get together the money to buy one.[2]

Thanks for your patience in going through all of this detail. It is unlikely that I will have another chance to communicate business with a naval architect and the temptation to get the most out of it is overwhelming. Enclosed is the second half of the design fee.

Sincerely,
David D. Hume

Bolger came back three weeks later with a new, crisp black ribbon in his typewriter. There was also a splendid side view of the completed vessel, marked with geometrical centers of the three sails and a total center of sail area labeled as 285 square feet. This was almost 15% more than I had thought the hull could carry and promised considerably better light air performance. It also assumed that the boat should be

---

[2]The mark's and dollar's gyrations, or some other cause, eventually led to the discontinuation of the importing of most of the engines I had looked at up to this point. Later, Bruce Rogers imported a shipment of 13 h.p. Vetus engines that are a combination of a Japanese block with Dutch injectors, electric gear and the like. It is a virtual clone of the Westerbeke and came as a package with batteries, controls, instruments and propeller for $2200, much the best price of anything that I was able to find. I still have the big, three-bladed prop hanging on the wall of my barn.

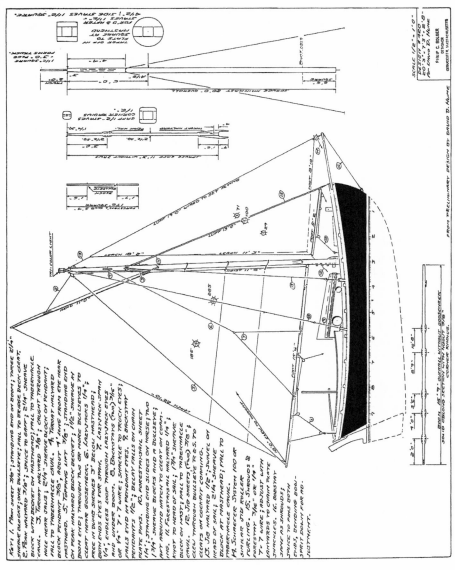

Specifications for standing and running rigging are included here as well as the dimensions and construction details of the spars.

reefed a little sooner as the wind piped up.

March 5, 1982

David D. Hume

Thanks for yours of Feb. 15. I try to write books in such a way as to inoculate against the "revealed truth" syndrome. I don't mind the tablets as long as they're lined up side by side so the inconsistencies can be noted.

I'm going to haul ahead and draw this up as soon as I can. I enclose the sail plan, which is as far as I've gotten. Rigging subject to alteration. Nothing in your last letter I have any objection to, unless you count the two portlights of differing sizes which for some reason doesn't look well to me but which are strictly an aesthetic matter of taste; i.e., I'll do it your way.[3]

The 4000-lb. displacement is what it would weigh if it floated like that, not, I hope, what it will weigh in fact. I trust it will float up a couple of inches. If you like, I'll figure approximately where I think it will float, guessing whether the last crew member to come aboard ate a banana first, but as we can't reduce the volume any there won't be much we can do about it. I'd say your estimate was not far out of the way. I guess you're right about the toilet. I had in mind that it would be used sitting well down inside, being infected with the common North American privacy neurosis, but the space is certainly very tight. The foot well isn't as bad as it looks, as the space above the engine hatch will be available, one reason I didn't show a bridge deck.

I'll put the hatch back off center. Centering it was a reflex. The compass may survive the proximity of the engine if

---

[3] Nautical writer Richard Henderson made this same observation about the port lights. When I got to finding the hardware, I discovered that the plan as originally drawn called for a 9" and a 5", one larger and the other smaller than I thought I had drawn. We ended up with a couple of standard Becton lights of 8" and 6" diameter, which to my eye, look pretty good and give a good view from inside. I also added a pair of 4" fixed lights in the front face of the house. The cabin is nice and light.

centered though mine is giving me fits at close to 6' from the Sabb. I have no better idea for yours.

There will be a hole back through the deadwood for the shaft to pass out through, though it's done so seldom I'd be tempted to drill the hole when and if needed. There's supposed to be room enough to get the prop off in the aperture.

Note here that by tinkering a little with the peaking of the gaff I got the mast proper, (not counting the truck which is just an extension of the top plug) down to twenty feet overall. This mast will be made up of four 1 1/2" staves so it won't check, with the taper taken off in flats.

Not sure I'd want the roller-furling jib myself, having once had a traumatic experience with one, but there's no harm in showing it. Alternative would be to have a sheave at the bowsprit end so the jib can be hauled inboard to be smothered. I think the running backstays can be left set up on both sides for windward work, and usually ties off to the shrouds on both sides off the wind.

Phil Bolger

March 11, 1982

Dear Phil Bolger,

Thanks for the comments and sail plan. The hull looks lovely and the spread of sail relatively enormous. Presumably she may move along, despite the chubby sections. With apologies for excessive kibitzing, a few further items come to mind.

1. Let's compromise the head location, i.e., aft of yours a bit, but forward of mine, so that climbing into the chamber one might find the seat to be about 12" below the deckline and a modicum of modesty preserved.

2. I had hoped to live without running backstays by fixing uppers to a chainplate about 12" aft of where you show it, on the assumption that this would let the boom swing out about 65° from the center line without rubbing and let the gaff swing off still more (80°?). I am probably wrong about this

and will defer to your judgement.

If both running backs are tied off before the wind, would the rig stay on the boat in case of an unexpected jibe? I could use ... a preventer, but this is hard to set up while hacking about dinghy-like in the river, or when being rolled by power boat wakes running back up the Connecticut on a summer Sunday afternoon.

3. Could we have a few more mast hoops?

4. Roller furling is probably best for the jib, but I might start with the sheave to save expense. Will the inner stay hold the mast by itself?

5. Is there an available fitting for the forward end of the staysail club to hold it up off the deck?

6. The truck should probably terminate in a tri-color lantern with some sort of pennant holder. I think Browning Aqua-signal makes one, but I haven't seen it. Such a mast head running light requires a couple of wires inside the mast since the hoops are on the outside. Staves should be glued so as to allow for a channel for wiring...

7. Please show location for some sort of anchor roller so we can leave a 15 lb. C.Q.R. rigged up, sufficiently outboard to allow the mud to be left until later.

8. You did not comment on my suggestion of positive buoyancy via styrofoam blocks built in. I have a 20 year-old son who just might try to cross the Davis Straight in this thing, so although I intend it as a coaster, offshore capability would make my mind easier.

Sincerely yours,
David D Hume

Two and a half weeks later a package of plans arrived with the next letter.

3/25/82

David D. Hume

Sorry to've been so long and still not finished. Its been giving me fits. But you can start laying her down from this and I hope I'll have the rest for you in a week or so. Plywood thickness, bottom, sides, and deck is 1/2" (double 1/4").

Your questions:

1.) Head and well etc. are the best I can do. I've had this erased and done over about five times. Maybe a better way will show when you have her set up.

2.) I think backstays are needed to set up luff of jib. Off the wind I don't think they're needed though there might be times when they'd be a comfort.

3.) I <u>hate</u> these great heaps of mast hoops. Only function of hoops is to keep sail from getting out of control while lowering. But sailmakers will be happy to give you twice as many or more.

4.) Inner stay will be ample support for the mast.

5.) I don't think any club fitting is needed. Just secure it to the foot of the sail.[4]

6.) The lantern at masthead might have a neat cap for a base that would also take the eyes for the halyards and backstays.

7.) Think with your light anchors you're better off without rotating sheaves on the bowsprit, but if wanted location will be same as dumb sheaves shown.

8.) Buoyancy foam is shown. Contrary to your comment, I doubt this would be much comfort in the Davis Strait, but could save your life in Long Island Sound. Batten it off plywood to some extent so it won't trap dampness more than can be helped.

Reverting to cockpit, I decided that in good weather the hatches could be open, with a platform over the engine for feet. In bad weather the small foot well should be adequate, and it doesn't make it possible to reach out to the sides as a

---

[4] I could never get it to set well until I finally (several years later) had a little goose neck made and screwed it down to the bowsprit.

longer well would.[5] Sorry about the location of the exhaust line. All I can say is that every other lead I thought of seemed worse. Wrap it up to hell and gone to avoid burning legs.

I think this has the makings of a spirited little sailer, and perfectly fit to go over the Davis Strait.

Phil. Bolger

P.S. Bottom is not a true conic shape, but it will take the p.w. O.K.

Another, larger envelope arrived ten days later, containing two complete sets of plans and a typed out set of scantlings and specifications keyed to reference numbers on the drawings. With them was the following note:

> Shout if you need more prints. I have an uneasy feeling you paid too much for it while I didn't get enough, but I think I've at least defined all the problems. Let me know how it goes....
>
> Phil. Bolger

14 April 1982

Dear Phil Bolger,

The final drawings are splendid. The combination of the contemporary and the ageless is all that I hoped for when we began. I say <u>we</u> because although you only learned of my contribution a few months ago, I had been reading your stuff and studying your plans for a number of years before I started to draw. Anyway, I love the way it all came out.

---

[5]This is one of the few sentences in PCB's entire correspondence the meaning of which I was unable to fathom. When he had the opportunity to read this manuscript he commented that he meant to write "<u>im</u>possible." That I had not already ascribed my confusion to his typo demonstrates another of the problems that arise from attributing the character of revealed truth to the emanations of mortal man. I wonder how many volumes of tortuous exegesis have been committed as the result of slips of the pens of James Joyce, Mao, Mr. Jefferson, or St. Paul.

Concerning your unease on the time it took, if Peter Duff liked it others might too. I have no objection to the design being sold to others although I'm under no illusion that it is likely to be the next generation's one design class, and what is very much of a swan to me might more probably be considered a duckling to other home builders. Anyway, if you want to put it in *Small Boat Journal* I would be delighted and flattered. It might, on the other hand, result in #2 being in the water before I am half way through the prototype. Lofting this weekend.

David

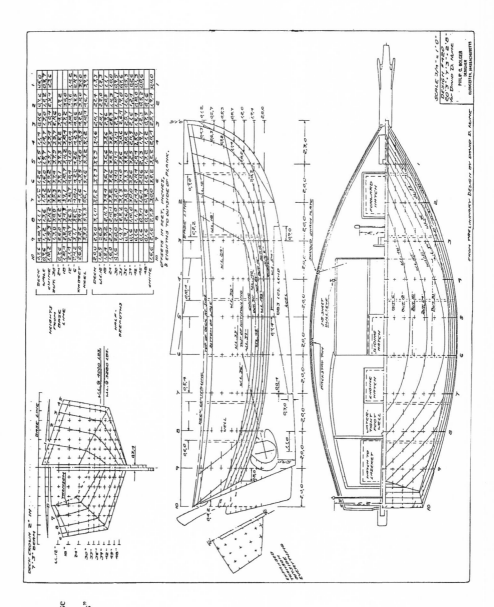

"Heights" in the table are measured down from the base line because the hull is built upside down. "Half Breadths" are measured out from the center line.

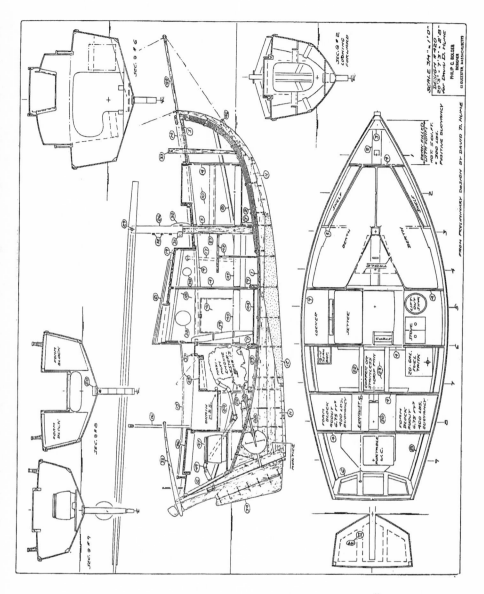

This drawing locates the interior arrangements quite precisely, but includes no dimensions since this work must be made to fit the hull as built from the lofted lines and final measurements must be made on the job.

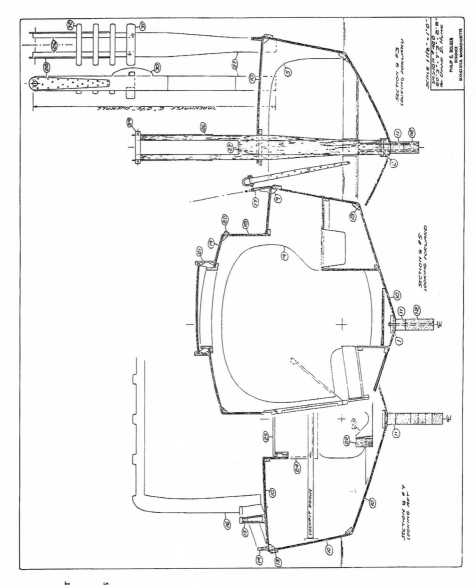

This drawing doubles the scale of the lines which allows clearer details of chines and hatches as well as serving as machinist's shop drawings to make patterns for the metal parts of the tabernacle and chain plates.

IV. *Building Blueberry*

Building a proper boat begins with more drawing, but this time on the floor and in full scale. I talked about the project with everyone I knew before starting and in the process caught the interest of Sam White, a former student of mine, who in the early 1980s had become an architect starting his practice in New York. The idea of drafting plans full scale, especially plans full of curves passing through innumerable points located by a "table of offsets" was a new experience for him and he was anxious to see how it was done. His genial enthusiasm led to his completing more than half the job.

We covered the greater part of the floor of a mini-gym on the second floor of Saint David's School with the thick mylar drafting film, twenty two feet long and eight feet wide. The mylar came with a pre-printed grid of 1/8" squares. Lofting offsets are generally expressed in feet, inches, and eighths, so most of the counting was already done for us. A half breadth of 6-5-4 translated to six feet, five and a half inches. We would put a dot on that station and go on to the next number. Eventually we connected the dots with twenty foot long strips of molding, holding them down with iron sash weights encased in oversized athletic socks to keep them in the proper curve until the line was traced off on the mylar. Over a long weekend, Bolger's drawing was enlarged sixteen fold, from being fifteen inches long in the original to something more than twenty feet. The curved lines had to be drawn fair; that is with no humps or swerves to force them through the points on the grid. In the case of a bump, fairness was to take precedence over the location of the dot: the hull had to have fair curves if the bent stringers and planking were to land on the transverse bulkheads that gave it its shape.

The necessary enlargement meant that each 1/16" on the drawing grew to be 1" on the boat. To figure his "offsets," the designer had to estimate eighths of sixteenths of an inch [.0078"] on the plan he drew. It is usual for some "fairing" to be done in the lofting, compromising the location of the dots. Amazingly enough, we found only a couple of points as much as 3/16" out of the middle of our lines, except for one that was an even foot wrong and was obviously a misread number. I mentioned this correction in a letter complimenting his draftsmanship almost a year later and got the following reply from Bolger:

> Thanks. I [have] corrected the bad offset. Frank Lloyd Wright said the Gods are jealous of plans with no mistakes (said he "neglected the precaution" once and came to grief).

To get the plan and profile views onto the mylar, we had to draw the one on top of the other, using different colored pencils; not as confusing as it sounds. Having the up and down distances of every point on the outside of the hull thus located in three dimensions, we were able to create a set of superimposed cross sections to use as patterns for the bulkheads. These crosswise members had to be made a half inch inside our lines to allow for the thickness of the plywood planking. Once this much smaller set of lines was done it turned out to fit on a piece of drafting film only four feet by five feet, the two halves of the hull being just flipped over copies of each other. The rest of the monster drawing was then rolled up and put away in the top of the barn where it still resides.

One final use of the big profile plan before consigning it to the upper part of the barn was to trace out the curve of the interior stem, a massive laminated member, curved like a giant's field hockey stick, that was to be the spine of the whole forward third of the boat. The stem was to be lami-

nated from quarter inch mahogany strips and was to finish 3"
thick and 5 1/2" wide. That meant that a dozen slabs of
mahogany, each 14 feet long, had to be coated with slippery,
gooey, epoxy resin (which would set up hard in something
like twenty minutes) and then wrestled into a set of forms
that would accurately define the curve Bolger had drawn on
the plan. They also had to be clamped together before the
resin set and protected from becoming permanently bonded
to the plywood floor under them by sheets of wax paper.

The first step was setting up joists for a level plywood floor
on which to build the hull. Since the barn timbers had been
in place since the late eighteenth century, this required a
number of shims and wedges. One end of the floor started
out nine inches lower than the other. Once a reasonably
level surface was built, a truly level center line was provided
by tightening a twenty foot length of 1 x 19 stranded rigging
wire between wooden blocks at either end and checking it
with a spirit level. This wire (left over from the shrouds of the
Penguin dinghy of many years before) became the datum
from which all other measurements were made. Vertical
locations above it were located with a plumb bob. Breadths
were measured out from the plumb line with a steel tape.

In the beginning of that first summer I had some help from
two of my sons, a couple of days each. But as the project wore
on through the years, it became more and more of a solo
effort. The five bulkheads of Bolger's design were cut out of
half inch luan[1] plywood and rimmed with 3/4" mahogany
stiffening frames. These assemblies were supplied with

---

[1]Luan is a tropical hardwood of reasonable durability that makes pretty good
plywood. It is sometimes called Philippine Mahogany but most of it is not from
the Philippines and it is not mahogany. Bruynzeel is better, but more expensive.
I used it for the cabin top and sliding hatch. The mahogany used for timber in
Blueberry is Honduras mahogany, known as "hondo" in the trade. It is first quality
boat building wood but long gone from Honduras and now imported from
farther south or from Asia where there are similar species.

temporary legs and stood up vertically along the center line. The keel apron planks and chine logs connected them and the structure stiffened appreciably. By mid-summer the curved lamination of the stem was slipped into the slots cut to receive it in the bulkheads. Sheer clamps and chine logs were mortised into the stem without too much damage and the blessed gap-filling quality of the thickened epoxy resin made up for my inaccuracies with a chisel. By August the whole frame of the hull seemed to have taken shape. Relatively massive floor timbers connected the midships bulkheads to the keel apron and presented broad surfaces to be glued to the hull planking. Then the beveling began.

Plywood will only bend in one direction at a time and if it was to lie down snugly on the frames, every edge had to be beveled to make a smooth fit from one frame to the next. These bevels were checked with a straight fairing batten in several directions. During the planing, I concluded that the chine logs had gotten so thin and deeply recessed into the bulkheads that they lacked the strength for their role. I doubled their thickness and refaired the resulting timber.

I built the frame for the transom by gluing the timbers to the cut-out plywood that would form the finished stern. The

resulting assembly was heavy and had to be located somewhere in the air where the various longitudinal members
came out in back of the last bulkhead. Since it was set at a
considerable angle to the rest of the bulkheads, it seemed
beyond the range of my ability in descriptive geometry to
locate it precisely. I measured it off the plans and even got out
the full scale lofting for comparison. In the end I hung it from
a sort of scaffold and tinkered it into place by sighting along
the keel apron and chines to see if it looked lined up right.
Judging by the finished hull, I guess I got it in the right place,
but at the time I had an odd sensation that the ship might have
a twisted, off-center rear end.

After a few last planing sessions in the week between
Christmas and New Year's with the wood stove roaring and
fluttering in the barn, I closed up shop for the season, drained
the pipes in the house and went back to New York until
spring. I was tired, and the simple process of splitting stove
billets for the barn heater left me short of breath; more so, it
seemed to me, than the effort warranted.

My older brother was a vascular surgeon who used to work
on hearts and I know what dyspnea is supposed to indicate,
so I called my doctor and asked for a check-up. Two cardi-
ologists later I was aware that I was a candidate for an early
heart attack from plugged up arteries, but also one that could,
perhaps, benefit from bypass surgery. I scheduled the operation into the narrow window of time between the Annual
Meeting of the Board of Trustees and Graduation, three and
a half weeks normally devoted to lots of symbolic activity
having to do with the completion of the school year. Several
hundred small boys got a chance to practice their epistola-
tory skills by writing speedy recovery letters to their headmaster.

The operation was less of a trial than even I, always opti-
mistic, had expected, but an ensuing sensation of profound
fatigue took some months to dispel. Mouth breathing and an

excessively heavy dose of antibiotics have a tendency to result
in a fungus infection with the old fashioned name of "thrush."
The sensation is one of having a wooden lining to the inside
of the mouth. Quite by accident, while still in the hospital, I
discovered that the only thing that really tasted good was
champagne. I tried all the Spanish and Australian varieties in
the weeks of recuperation. By midsummer I was back in fair
shape and got the boat planked in the two layers of quarter
inch luan, even working out the mysterious connection
along the chine between the stem and the foremost bulkhead
where the planking changed from overlapping to butting
together. This nice little detail isn't much noticed by people
who haven't tried joining the edges of plywood as they
change along such a twisty junction. Glenn L. Witt has
written a book on boatbuilding in plywood which has a
couple of pages on it. Worth the twenty-five bucks from
International Marine Publishers, since I wouldn't have begun to know how to get the joint right without some
instruction. Most things about boat building can either be
figured out from common sense or found in a good book.
Most of the books can be found at International Marine.[2]

Not being in top form after the chest surgery, I hired
genial and burly Ben Griffin, then a teen-aged neighbor, for
part of the summer. He operated as a sort of mobile set of
vise-grips, slinging around one end of the plywood panels or
another and wrestling them onto the frame. The hull got
planked and the keel and deadwood were built up on top of
the inverted whale by bolting on a seemingly endless stack of

---

[2]Call them for nothing at 1-800-822-8158. They will send you a wonderful
catalogue and you will be well down the ways toward perdition. The most
essential book for me was *The Gougeon Brothers on Boat Construction*. Watch out
for instruction manuals that assume that virtue is only to be found in mid-
nineteenth century methods of construction. Among the old timers, Sam Rabl is
best, if you can find a copy of his *Boatbuilding in Your Own Back Yard*. Alas, it seems
to be out of print.

fir two by fours and fairing the cracks between their edges
with *BONDO*, the auto body shop plastic filler that Noah
recommended for the job. Space for the keel casting was
occupied temporarily by a plywood box of appropriate shape
that was later to be used as a form for casting the ballast.
Drilling through the stacked 2 x 4's, hoping to hit the floor
timbers square on gave a few thrills. About the second hole
attempted got out of line and the auger came out through the
side of the keel. The mishap was surprisingly easy to fix. An
appropriately sized dowel was lubricated with epoxy and
banged into place with a mallet. It set up in fifteen minutes
and I planed off the part that came through the side. Lots of
sanding and many more coats of resin followed. By the time
that cold weather shut down the yard for another season, the
smoothly epoxied hull glowed under the barn lights like a
small wooden whale, beached in the old Connecticut barn.

I wrote triumphantly to Bolger to tell him how things had
gone. I included some speculation on appropriate names for
the vessel, now that it was beginning to look as though it
would float if turned right side up in a pond. I also had the
temerity to confess that I had departed from his plans to the
extent of having left out the chine battens he had drawn
fitting tight up to the edges of the plywood. I had simply
overlapped the planks on the double thick chine logs I had
installed and gave the whole thing a smooth inch and a half
radius. I counted on the epoxy to keep the edge grain of the
plywood sealed. After five years in the water, I have so far no
reason to regret this joint. Most of the gloomy things said
about plywood[3] are handed down from boatbuilders of a
prior era, before Bruynzeel and before epoxy resins. A hull
glued up from two convex laminations, as *Blueberry*'s is, is
really a cold molded plywood *monocoque* and has immense
strength and durability.

---

[3]The legendary Nathaniel G. Hereshoff said it "was always disappointing, and
sometimes came apart."

All the names I suggested were two part or two word titles, allowing for the division on either side of the rudder and stern post. Bolger followed the format by suggesting *PERSEV-ERENCE* [sic] or rather "PERSEV| |ERENCE" as being appropriate. Yet, I was still only two years into the project and the shell of the hull was done.

Seven months later I wrote to him again to ask for another couple of sets of prints. The originals were tattered and had begun to fade from exposure to daylight. I also asked him for details of rudder gudgeons and pintels, and mentioned the name "Blueberry" for the first time. It had been suggested by my wife in contrast to my idea of "Cranberry." She said she wouldn't want to go sailing on a red boat.

Bolger's answer had numbered paragraphs and pen sketches of the heavy sheet metal fittings for the rudder. He concluded by saying:

> Make cardboard patterns on the hull, and feel free to exercise invention....I like *Blueberry*. Still like your design too, which can't be counted on.

The summer of 1984 saw the parturition of the blue hull from the barn, the building of a semi-permanent cradle upside down on top of it and, eventually, the inversion of the whole thing on the grass. Another neighbor's boy, Jody James, who had been mowing the lawn on his father's mini-tractor since he was nine, joined the project at the age of twelve.

I cut out a pair of semicircles from 3/4 inch builder's plywood and fastened them to the frame underneath (on which the boat had been built) and also to the new cradle frame on top. This structure was sculptured to fit the curves of the hull and padded with old carpet scraps. Once the whole thing seemed reasonably rigid, we urged it out of the barn on rollers made of sections of steel pipe, jacked it up to a small angle from the horizontal and wedged in a couple of props. A strong nylon mooring pennant was led over the hull to a "come-along" which we tied to a tree. Jody levered the winch while I watched anxiously. Quite slowly and easily, the whole thing rolled over on the wooden half wheels and came to rest with a polite thump on the grass.

Building the inside of a boat is a little like making a dollhouse, something I had essayed in prior years. The project is made simpler if you can still stand up inside without cracking your head, so I put off deck and cabin top for as long as

possible. In went a cabin sole, bunks on frames with lockers beneath, the settee, the galley dresser, a twelve-gallon aluminum fuel tank, and eventually a husky chunk of timber drilled to make the shaft log. A neighboring professional boat builder, Gary Weissenberger, was persuaded to join the project for a couple of half days to set up the engine beds. These are relatively massive timbers, laminated to be three inches thick and in places as much as eight inches deep. They are held down with half inch bronze lag bolts let into the floor timbers.

The lead casting for the keel was produced from my pattern by a boat yard which was turning out top secret lead wings for the keels of twelve-meter sailboats destined to lose the cup to Australia that season. It weighed just shy of 900 pounds and required some ingenuity to get it out of the back of my pickup truck. It came from the casting quite rough and I attacked it with both hand and power planes to smooth out the sides. Eventually it was coated with the ever useful epoxy resin and looked quite slick. Getting it under the boat and up into its recess in the keel was a late autumn job. The only help at hand was Amity, a nursing student on vacation for the moment. With the help of an ancient Datsun jack and a bunch of wooden wedges we got it in, more or less straight. After drilling down from the inside, through the keel apron, floor timbers and wooden fin, Jody and I banged home nine long bronze rods, each a half inch in diameter, hand threaded on the ends and equipped with washers and nuts. These bolts were "lubricated" with epoxy when they went in, which is probably not the right way to do it, but I think they will stay where they are for the forseeable future.

The graduation of our two youngest, Noah (Mechanical Engineering) and Amity (Nursing) made an immediate and massive change in our domestic economy. Money discovered in the family bank account not destined to be spent on college tuition is *real* money, like a raise on which no income tax need be paid. A summer trip to Scotland and the purchase of the power plant for *Blueberry* were the immediate results.

The Vetus engine was shipped to New York where I could count on being home to receive it from a trucker and where I knew I could find help to wrestle it in from the street. Breaking the packing down into components would make for lighter work in moving it to Connecticut. The freight bill maintained that the crate contained better than 220 pounds, but the engine itself was advertised at 160. Unpacked in the

front hall of the school, the engine sat on wooden skids in the
Nursery School coat room for a week. It was painted bright
yellow and gleamed with nifty fittings. The four-year-olds
studied and patted it and became happily familiar with the
sight and feel of a diesel engine. I eventually brought the
pickup truck to New York and, with help, got the beautiful
thing situated in the back. On the way up I-95 I noticed that
the added weight in the rear made the truck ride more
smoothly than ever before. I did not notice, however, that the
silky ride disguised the speed of the vehicle and the first of the
Thanksgiving weekend troopers pulled me over in Milford
to say that the radar had figured that I was doing 83 in a 55
mph zone.

The smallest Vetus engine is a version of the 10 h.p.
Westerbeke design and Bolger had already commented on
that engine favorably. His letter said that one had been
installed in a fantail launch that he had designed.

> I came down to the wharf, late for the launching, and they
> ran her past at good speed, not two boat lengths from where
> I stood. All I could hear was the bow wave, and the wave is
> not very noisy in that hull either.

May of 1986 brought a further exchange of letters.

Dear Phil Bolger,
    Spring having returned, I dutifully report to you, being
accountable to no one else except conscience and the pursuit
of pleasure. Perhaps the most difficult thing about recreational
boat building is the managing of motives. It is also, in my case,
a textbook case of living with the deferral of gratification—
I am well into the fifth year of the project....

The answer was characteristically prompt.

Dear David,

Thanks for the progress report. She certainly looks elegant, "yacht finish." Just had the plans out and still like it myself. Good thing about conservative design is that you're not so likely to change your mind about it before it gets built!...

By that Thanksgiving the interior of the cabin and the engine installation were complete. The overhead of the cabin was painted right side up and then installed as the deck, upside down. The custom metal work of the massive tabernacle plates was undertaken by Jerry Boisvert at his Ace Machine Works in Salem, Connecticut, just up the road from my house. As the project got on to such custom items, I became increasingly glad that I no longer was financing the education of our own young; for a brief moment in time, all six were gainfully employed. A technical question about the gooseneck for the boom written on my Christmas card brought a few characteristic comments from Bolger:

> You could probably fake something up out of eye-bolts or something, as the requirements aren't all that stringent. What they used to do.
>
> Are you going to feel that all purpose has gone out of your life when you finish her?
>
> Phil

Another set of seasons came and went in New York and in Connecticut. The sheet metal stove descended from the barn loft in October and the pipes were strung together with the hanging loops of last year's bailing wire. By the following May the whole apparatus was disassembled again and the pipes and stove hauled back up to the top of the barn to make more room on the building floor. I added a drill press to the band saw and other tools in my collection and acquired several dozen more clamps. My report to the eminence in Gloucester summed it up.

9 September 1987

Dear Phil,

Well, the sixth summer passed in a spray of spruce chips and a gallon or two of Gougeon's best epoxy to glue up the staves of the mast and laminate the rudder. That blade weighs about 50 lbs and is hung on some nice ss#316 hardware I drew up from the small scale shown on your plan and had them made by a local machine shop....The toe rails were a hell of a job to bend in two directions and I never did get them down quite tight so I filled the gap with W.E.S.T. goop and the whole thing seems as rigid as a railroad track. I was a bit more successful in having a hair line joint on the cap rails on the cockpit coaming, although the 1" teak was pretty inflexible even when bending in only one direction (vertical). I ended up wedging 2 x 4s between the rail and the loft rafters while the glue was kicking and using a number of ss. screws countersunk into the blocks inside the coamings....

The mast turned out to be much easier than I had imagined. I had the lumber man joint the faying surfaces of the Sitka and it all went together fine. I even got a piece of lead (cast from the keel trimmings) built in below the pin where the thing is reinforced with a glued in block of Hondo to take the wear of that <u>huge</u> pin you specified. Wires to lantern and antenna are grooved around the blocks and lead. The tapered top section is reinforced with 20" of mahogany inside the thin-walled top. Cabin top went on in September before Labor Day...Thos. Clark of Essex is doing sails at great cost but they should be pretty and durable, what with all those oversewn grommets for the lacing.

Launch date should be in mid to early August 1988.

Sincerely
David

Later I sent a post card in which I asked his opinion of "naturally" finished, or unfinished, teak. I also asked what a <u>cavel</u> was, having been unable to find the word in the *Oxford Concise*. I could tell from the plans that they were some sort of cleats on the back of the tabernacle to which one could secure the halyards. I also knew by then that Bolger would have an opinion, possibly unorthodox, on any subject.

> Dear David,
>   Cavel is a corrupt spelling, which I will forthwith cease using, for KEVEL. See Webster, <u>much</u> the best dictionary for nautical terms, including any specialized dictionaries and glossaries I ever came across....
>   Thanks for the news...on the teak, if it was mine, I'd either varnish it, or paint it and try to forget that it was teak. The weathered teak just looks neglected to me.
>   I'll look forward to the launching.
>   Phil

Lacking the twenty pound unabridged third edition, I stuck to the definition derived from an inspection of Bolger's plans.

Work progressed rapidly on spring weekends and in June. *Blueberry* came out of the barn on July 3rd, 1988, her cabin hatch, tabernacle, gallows frame and other vertical projections yet to be permanently fastened after the rest of the ship cleared the lintel of the barn doors. All was assembled the next day and she flew her colors for the first time on the national holiday. I sent Bolger a sheaf of color photographs of the little ship sitting on the lawn. He answered:

> Thanks for the note and photos. She looks nice! And one thing about a timeless design like that; you're not apt to wish you'd known then what you know now, (there's a steel ketch

near San Francisco that's been building for about fifteen years, is now nearly finished, and I wish etc.)....

Phil

The actual completion of the boat called for a party, presumably at the launching. But it would have been impossible for me to both launch the boat and act as the host. A christening on the lawn at home was decreed with the principal in her cradle, sails rigged and new paint gleaming in the afternoon sunshine. I drew up an invitation from Bolger's sail plan and we invited forty or fifty friends from both Salem and New York.

CATHERINE AND DAVID HUME
Request the honor of your company at the Christening of

BLUEBERRY

5:00 PM

SATURDAY 30 JULY, 1988
(RAIN DATE : SUNDAY 31 JULY)

340 DARLING ROAD
SALEM CONNECTICUT

Along with attorneys, artists, musicians, neighbors, some-time helpers on the project, there were professors, lawn mowers, Bob Vaill, our trashman, Jody, Ben, and various members of their and our extended families, as well as feisty and smiling little Lois Darling. There was plenty to eat and drink and one prize bottle of G. H. Mumm's most specially reserved cuvée received as an unlooked for present from some grateful school parent some years before. It was much too expensive a wine to smash over the bow, and besides, I was not going to chance disfigurement of the ship by knocking it about with a hard glass bottle. We popped the cork and Cathy poured a modicum of bubbly over the varnished white oak bowsprit while telling her and the company that she was christened "Blueberry!" I shared the rest with the other helpers and the party went on until almost dark.

By this date, Jody James was ready for college and had become a rugged and muscular young man as well as a championship diver. Shortly before I lost him to the engineering school at Carnegie-Mellon, I was able to press him into service for some of the large muscle activity associated with getting the boat into the water. John Leonard of Cove Landing Marine brought up his boat-moving trailer with hydraulic props and we disassembled the cradle in stages as we worked the moveable arms under the hull. We made the inland voyage down to the Cove without incident and settled the boat alongside the dock to the approving glances of a half dozen people who were sworn to keep the secret if she didn't float close to her designed waterline.

All went well; that is until the first live test of the engine. For some inexplicable reason it snorted and stalled after each start, all the while belching and burbling out through the cooling water *intake* port under the hull. It was as though the whole cooling system was operating backwards. The water pump was disassembled twice and black and greasy water sprayed liberally around the galley. Almost no water came out of the exhaust port in the transom, but I did notice a bit of string hanging from the tail pipe. We left the boat at the dock and I went home to sleep on the problem.

All through the construction of *Blueberry* I had come up against things that I did not directly see how to do. I would take these to bed with me and go right on building, both in sleep and wakefulness. Usually, by morning, I had successfully built the part of the boat under consideration in my mind and it only remained to repeat the steps on the following morning to complete the job. The case of the backwards cooling system was no exception. *Something* had to be plugging up the exhaust line and the expelled gasses were coming back through the heat exchanger, blowing their way past the rubber impeller blades of the water pump and the raw water strainer to exit through the hull fitting whence the cooling water was supposed to enter.

That string in the tail pipe was the clue. How much more of it was there, and where?

I was up by six the next morning and had the cockpit sole removed in short order to get at the waterlock muffler. When I got it free of its hose clamps and out on deck, the problem became clear. The muffler was full, packed full of wet string, mop lint and upholstery stuffing. The engine and its fittings had been installed two years earlier in the ancient country barn. When we moved back to New York, the mice too came into winter quarters and found nothing so snug as the dry compartment at the end of the long exhaust tube in the boat sitting handy on the stocks in their barn. I was reminded of the Rat's conversation with the field mice in *The Wind in the Willows* when they explain to him that they must move back into town early because the best flats are taken quite soon and then one has to put up with *anything*.

I cleaned out the soggy junk with a straightened coat hanger and reassembled the cockpit sole. The engine ran beautifully on the first try. By lunch time the boat was rigged and the sails bent on. I set out for the first sea trial with new friend Worth Holden (a reliable seaman) as crew.

Everything worked perfectly. We all went sailing every day for a week.

I wrote to Phil Bolger again after our return to New York for the new school year, my thirty-sixth as Headmaster of Saint David's School.

10 September 1988

Dear Phil,

Now that the wonderful month of August has been fulfilled and school must keep once more, I need to take a moment to write to you. *Blueberry* is all that I had hoped and more. Although I have not yet sailed her in a real breeze of wind, she behaves quite splendidly in all the conditions met so far. In a steady, light southwesterly in the Sound with thwartships schock cord hooked in a wooden jam on the underside of the tiller, she steers herself for several minutes at a time. A sheet to tiller rig would be better of course. Stability and comfort are fine and the great set of fence posts of that gallows are great for leaning against when standing on deck on a reach or a beat. An overnight up the Niantic River solo was pleasant and all life support systems are more than adequate ...

I enclose pictures... [taken] in the Connecticut River, south of Brockway channel between Hamburg Cove and Deep River.

Blueberry draws favorable comment and thumbs up signs wherever we have gone. Everybody wants to know who designed and built her. I modestly attach my name to yours while acknowledging the applause. This weekend we will be at a traditional boat gathering at the Connecticut River Museum at Essex.

Total success of happy client of great designer. I will send the better picture to *Woodenboat* for their "Launchings" column. I wonder if they will have the wit to publish it.[4]

Sincerely,
David

---

[4] They did, Jan/Feb issue, 1989, #86, page 100, together with a complimentary little squib about her construction.

V. *Early Sailing*

WHEN I was very little, my family "went to the shore" at Westhampton, Long Island. We spent the latter part of August and the week after Labor Day there *in illo tempore*, from the days before I was aware of where I was until the famous season of 1938 when the great New England hurricane made an inlet of what had been the West Bay Bathing Station. Thus began the metamorphosis of Westhampton from a conservative summer beach town to whatever it has become by this time. We stayed at the Apaukuck Point House each summer for those two or three weeks until after I turned nine. I remember it as a large and amply fenestrated building, cream with dark green trim without and with white painted iron bedsteads and small white cotton rugs on the bare floors inside. No liquor was served even after prohibition had been gone for a number of years, but people held cocktail parties in their rooms and invited other guests. The host couple was, as a result, a few minutes late for the *table d'hôte* dinner served promptly at seven o'clock. When they entered the dining room they were applauded by their erstwhile guests. Young men wore striped blazers and smoked pipes. There was a dock reaching out into the bay and sailboat races on weekends, but I never went to sea in those waters.

As much the youngest of three brothers I developed a keen sense of competition that was little ameliorated by the happy companionship of my younger sister, Zonni. She was fun to play with, but the obvious desirability of greater age and just plain masculinity pressed me on to emulate all that Michael and Stephen undertook. I never was able to adjust completely to the ratios of our ages, they being separated by just fourteen

83

months, and I being more than two years younger. The result
was that when they took tennis lessons together, Zonni and
I were still playing croquet. In the year in which they got
tuxedos for Christmas to go to fashionable dancing classes in
New York, I was presented with a Hallicrafter short wave
radio. I really feel that I got the better of that deal, but it did
serve to make me feel the need to compete still more fiercely
in whatever way I could.

Most of this energy went into verbal activity. I read almost
everything my brothers put down for a moment, including
books that were considered "too old for him." A subscription
to *Popular Science* (probably designed to divert my attention
from yet another adult privilege allowed to Michael and
Stephen) had the result of equipping me with a vast accumu-
lation of facts. Discarded geography texts found in the attic
and some abridgements of the novels of Jules Verne added to
my store of eclectic and randomly assorted information. I
also developed a disproportionately large vocabulary, much
of which I was unable to spell, and some of which, being a
nonphonetic, visual reader, I could not pronounce with any
degree of accuracy even though I knew how to use the words
well enough.

One thing I lacked above all was an extra-familial friend of
similar taste and ability. At twelve and thirteen I ached for the
acceptance of a peer. Even when this was found only fleet-
ingly, the time was sweet and the experiences rememberable
at a distance of half a century.

By the early 1940s our late summer seaside rustication had
migrated to Martha's Vineyard and eventually to Chatham
on Cape Cod. On one of my first afternoons there I walked
out onto the dock of the Stage Harbor Yacht Club and
watched the preparation for racing the local class of 14-foot
sloops, Spaulding Dunbar's Catabouts. This boat was a
sturdy little sailer with a large cockpit, a cuddy that provided

dry storage and even crouching shelter, and, in spite of the name, a fair sized jib. Like all other boats on the shores of Cape Cod, it had a centerboard rather than a keel and depended for ballast on the weight of the crew, kept as far to windward as possible. The day was a windy one and most of the boats had three kids aboard, some even four. As I watched, a bright yellow boat luffed up to the dock and the boy holding the mainsheet called to me.

"Hey kid! Do you want to crew?"

I was on board in the instant before the boat bore off the wind again and learned the names of my new shipmates. Dick was the owner of the vessel, but Patty was the skipper for the race, being acknowledged to be one of the finest helmsmen[1] in the fleet. Wedged in forward of the centerboard trunk along with me was another boy of my own age, Louie Gilbert. For some reason the jib sheet was given only a half turn around a cleat and it took the combined grip and heave of both Louie and me to keep it trimmed flat enough to satisfy Patty and Dick. I can't remember how we finished in the race, but Louie and I had established some sort of correspondence by the time we pried our deeply grooved hands from the manilla line that held that jib in its proper airfoil shape.

Louie, like all of the kids who summered in Chatham, was a sailor, but he also, like me, confronted the world in largely verbal terms. He wrote a weekly newspaper called the *Chatham Chatter* which he reproduced on an even then ancient mimeograph machine. The paper ran advertisements (charged at some unknown rate) and sold for three cents a copy. I was in awe and admiration of both his editorial and entrepreneurial skill.

---

[1]In those more innocent days, although girls practiced *seamanship*, we felt quite distinguished in that the Commodore of our yacht club was *Mrs.* McClay.

I sailed with Louie several times that summer. I don't suppose we spent more than five afternoons together, but for the time that was, he was a most satisfactory friend. He was understanding of the novice, friendly to the newcomer, and able to delight in the exercise of our mutually extensive vocabulary and store of miscellaneous information.

The Labor Day weekend was a windy one and Louie wanted to sail his own boat in the regatta at the SHYC. It had, however, no classmates in Stage Harbor, for Louie owned an ancient Cotuit Skiff, a boat indigenous to a town thirty miles to the west of us. The fashionable young people in Chatham all sailed Catabouts, the seniors Baybirds, the rich had Monomoys (another, larger Dunbar design), and the young-sters sailed Beetle Cats. Our boat, for Louie had asked me to crew, was handicapped in with the Beetles. The only trouble with this was that the Cotuit Skiff had an enormous gaff-headed sail supported by a 12 1/2-foot-hull with little more than half the beam of the Beetle. In theory we were endowed with the ability to outsail them on any point of the wind, but in actuality we would have to reef far sooner and needed much more live ballast to keep on our feet in a blow.

There were no spare kids on the dock that afternoon and Louie and I set out for the starting line already well soaked by the spray of a wind that was besting 20 knots. We did well at the start and were still in the race as we entered the second round of the markers, although we knew that we had to give away an outrageous amount of time to the Beetle Cats as a result of the handicapping of our sail area. As we neared the nun at the far end of the harbor, our angle of heel began to approach a critical 45°. The skiff had no side decks and the water stayed out of the boat mostly because of my hanging out over the windward gunwale. The shallow "barn door" rudder was lifted by our angle of heel and began to lose its grip on the water. The boom was a long one and extended a good three feet beyond the transom. Our speed was phenomenal, but our ability to alter course was becoming problematic. The rudder turned uselessly in the foam of our wake. Letting off the sheet resulted in the end of the boom and the clew of the sail going into the water, tripping her up and driving our bow farther off the wind. Finally we just sailed her right under and ended up swimming around trying to right the boat and get the sail off her.

We were retrieved by a Coast Guard launch detailed to watch the race. Louie protested that their methods of salvage would do irreparable damage to the old hull, all to no avail. We were put aboard another boat manned by some adults while the launchmen yanked Louie's boat about, sprung its mast partners, cut a line or two, pumped it out with an engine connected to a fire hose, and eventually deposited it on the beach near the Yacht Club. In those days the USCG was supposed to "help" anyone in distress on the water, but they were not noted for the delicacy of their seamanship or the gentleness with which they handled small boats.

Louie's boat did not recover from that race that year and I don't recall where he was the following summer, but I still remember the brief friendship with great fondness.

In subsequent years we chartered a Baybird for the time we spent in Chatham. It had a big "42" on her mainsail but no name on her transom. We were told it was called "Tattoo" but we never referred to her as that. Another nameless sloop we took on for a week in Chatham we designated *NEMO* for the wordplay Ulysses used to deceive Polyphemus.

Sailing the Baybird taught Michael and Stephen quite a lot about managing a sailboat and how to get in and out of trouble. Being the youngest, I got few chances to take the helm. We once managed to put her over in an unexpected jibe and came close to losing our father by throwing him a seat cushion that had been perverted from its purpose as a flotation device by being filled with sand so that it could be used as moveable ballast. He managed to let it sink to the bottom without taking him with it. His gold Tiffany pocket watch was the only real casualty of the incident. Capsizing a small boat in Stage Harbor was considered more of a matter for amused comment than a disaster; the boats were all buoyant, being made of wood in those days, and the harbor was so shallow that you could walk to shore from most locations. The low-lying beaches, Hardings and Monomoy Point[2] protected Stage Harbor from the seas that worked up in Vineyard Sound outside, but the wind blew just as strongly inside as out. The combination of small waves and large winds made for some exciting sailing.

Chatham was a place of wonder in that time. It smelled of seaweed, salt and wild roses. The wind was almost constant but the late summer water was warm. The space under the decks or in the cuddies of the small boats smelled of marlin, which is, I guess, the aroma of the Stockholm tar which impregnates the twisted Italian hemp that sailors have used for generations to tie almost anything to anything else very securely. The clean and piquant saltiness of that tar lingers in old boat sheds and in the lockers of cabins. In a fiberglass yacht it can even mask the aroma of slow curing resin. To this day the smell is like Proust's famous cookie to me. It moves me back in time to these early experiences of late childhood in boats on Cape Cod.

But by then most of the world was already at war and Michael was soon in the NROTC at college. The Pearl Harbor attack came that winter. In the following summer we hung blankets over the windows at dusk to reduce the sky glow against which the U Boats could see the silhouettes of ships off the Atlantic coast.

---

[2]Now called Monomoy Island, being separated from the mainland by one of the later hurricanes of the 1950s.

All three of us joined the Navy during the war, but as usual for the younger brother, I missed the opportunity to go to sea. My service was as a land bound Disbursing Storekeeper during the demobilization after the Japanese surrendered.

But the urge to sail, to be on the water, to own or even build a boat was there under the skin. I was brought up on tales from both sides of my family that directed my attention to the sea. Thomas J. Hume, my grandfather, once kept a 43-foot centerboard yawl in the upper East River when the family lived on 93rd Street before the turn of the century. As a younger man he had made a voyage of unknown purpose with several fellows from New York harbor to Apalachicola, Florida in the late autumn of 1872. The boat, described only as the "Sloop Yacht Argo," put to sea under double reefs on November first in a strong Northwest wind. He kept an accurate log which notes the passing of Sandy Hook light at 6:35 AM and records the times of a number of landmarks along the way with similar precision. After the Highland lights, Barnegat, and Little Egg harbor, they sighted Cape May light at 8:45 PM and dropped anchor an hour later. Figuring this distance as 120 nautical miles gives an average speed of close to nine knots. Since the best speed of a displacement hull is close to 1.34 times the square root of the waterline length of the vessel, *Argo* works out to be around 45 feet on the water. Considering the lines of yachts of the time, she must have been close to 60 feet over all and almost surely had a bowsprit beyond that. Now *that's* a proper yacht, although in 1872 it was surely considered small.

My great-grandfather David DesJardins, however, was a mariner and a ship builder on an altogether different scale. He lived in the now extinct village of Pointe-Séche near Kamouraska on the St.Lawrence River in the Province of Quebec. He followed his father into ship building and several times built "goélettes (petits naivres á deux mâts) et des grands trois-mâts." Their idea of a little two-masted schooner was probably about 70 to 80 feet. Three-masted schooners of the period were of a minimum length of 120 feet on deck and some were as great as 150. It is worth recollecting that adding thirty or forty to the length of a boat doesn't change the ends much, but extends the middle, the heavy and bulky part of the hull. Like any cubic or three-dimensioned object, a boat grows in size and displacement by the *cube* of the linear dimension. Thus *Amelia*, the largest of the DesJardins schooners, was really more than eight times the size of *Argo*. An account of her building exists somewhere in the family history. The timbers were cut from the forest within a few miles of the farm and boat yard. They were sawn,

steamed, and fastened in place with treenails at the home of her maker. It took three years to build her, less than half as long as *Blueberry*, starting in 1864. She sailed the Atlantic to Liverpool and the coast of Brazil for many successful voyages until a great storm shattered her bowsprit and carried away much of her rigging. She made Baltimore, however, without loss of life. DesJardins repaired her with new masts and bowsprit, but he then retired from the sea and sent *Amelia* to Europe again under the command of two of his sons, Arsène and David, aged twenty-eight and twenty-two. Off Saint-Pierre-et-Miquelon they met a hurricane. The narrator records that "la mer ne ramena acune épave, acun cadavre," neither flotsam nor body. The date of the disaster was just two years after T. J. Hume's successful pleasure voyage in much the same waters. The DesJardins probably set out earlier in the season and managed to catch one of the tropical storms that Hume missed by leaving in November.

Although my wife thinks that my involvement with boats has a deep atavistic component, something connected to the DNA that formed brain and bowels, I really think that anyone given the proximity of an accessible harbor and a shed to build in, will sooner or later undertake a raft, a skiff, a shallop. Still, for me it might never have come about had it not been for the friend who gave us that semi-derelict Penguin Dinghy.

VI. *The End of the Season*

A LL SAILS begin alike from the home port. Park the pickup truck; carry the bag of ice down to the dock; stow it in the cooler. Start up the engine; cast off the docking lines. Depending on the tide, either sweep off in a grand curve or jog back and forth to get turned around in the channel until we are headed west, towards the narrows between the Inner and Outer Cove. Past Eliot Clarke's dock, I set up the Autohelm and let it steer *Blueberry* until I am almost on Jonathan Jewett's dock, past the little nun off the end of the Camp Clare beach. Thence correct course 30° to port for Al Hine's dock and start to cast off the sail stops.

All these maneuvers are preprogrammed. Rather like the first half dozen moves on a chess board, they fall into the familiar pattern of a known opening: the light air in the southwest opening; the brisk northwesterly gambit; or the grey east wind beginning. But, also like chess, the variations increase exponentially by the minute, and by the time the boat has reached the mouth of the Cove and enters the River, the experience is unique. Last September I contrived to put *Blueberry* aground on the bar in the middle of the river, just north of the mouth of the Cove—something I had never done before, a truly new adventure.

But *Blueberry* was designed with occasional groundings in mind. The keel "drags" aft, that is it gets to be deeper until the greatest draft is just in front of the rudder post which is built to require a little less water and thus stay out of trouble from contact with the bottom. After all Bolger's concern about the little boat settling by the stern with a crew in the cockpit, it is useful to note that the opposite is also true; removing the crew from the cockpit raises the stern of the boat appreciably. My usual technique for getting off the bottom worked in this case. The engine is started at medium throttle in reverse and the crew then proceeds forward to the bowsprit. A few hundred pounds of live weight out over the stem will raise the stern a good three inches, usually plenty to detach the boat from the shoal and allow the Vetus to back her off.

Backing off from a grounding is another of my grandfather's nautical maxims: always get off the same way you got on. That one is a little like my mother-in-law's injunction to her daughter that she should always come home from the party with the same boy that she went with. Many of these caveats and instructions have near universal applications. "Always shorten sail before you have to," is one that is hard to appreciate until after the experience of waiting five minutes too long, wondering how soon it would be before those black clouds gathering to windward would require you to tie in a reef or drop the main altogether. A hundred years ago the yachtsmen of Long Island Sound, like my grandfather, had little else to go on other than the rhymes about the weather, the appearance of the clouds, the temperature of the air and the more or less reliable indications of the aneroid barometer. There were no N.O.A.A. weather broadcasts, fewer navigational markers, no VHF radios with which to question other people on the water. Even Captain Geo. Eldridge's *Tide and Pilot Book* was in its infancy, and the pattern of currents at the various stages of the tide was mostly a matter of local knowledge. They also lacked auxiliary engines and carried such hair-raising additions to their rigs as jackyard topsails to give them just that last tad more ability to catch a dying breeze on the way home. Their greatest margin of safety lay in a large anchor and a long rode.

Heading on up the river towards Joshua Rock, I was reassured to note that the Coast Guard had marked the east side of that mid-river shoal with a new green buoy, the first new navigational marker in the River in years. Maybe the edge of the shoal had migrated out to where *Blueberry* met it.

Whether you can make Joshua Rock on three or four tacks up the river or not is always a question. The combination of wind and tide is never quite what it was the last time: another variation following the predictable beginning. And the seasons change too. In early June the lower story of the eastern river bank foliage was thick with the pink and white blossoms of the mountain laurel. You have to have your boat in early in the season to enjoy this spring treat, the blooming of the Connecticut state flower. The spring also brings the last of the winter's spoil downstream to Long Island Sound. Small logs, branches, and a few full-sized trees move slowly south in the current. Not many of them, but enough to require a sharp look out.

Windless days on the flood tide also bring the bluefish up the river. Sometimes they are solitary and jump a foot or more from the water with a great smack and an enlarging circle of ripples. On one occasion I saw them pursuing smaller bait fish, alewives perhaps, in a great shoal. The small fry leaped out of the water in groups of thirty or more, desperately trying to stay ahead of the voracious blues. Two twelve-year-old boys in a rowboat were scooping up the prey with a crab net. I didn't see them take any of the larger predators. Once in a while I have witnessed an osprey making his elegant pickup with outstretched talons, snagging a fish of almost his own weight and wrestling his burden into the air for the trip back to the navigational light tower where he has built his home of twigs and driftwood sticks.

The Great Blue Heron is one of the landed gentry of the riverbank. They stand tall and aristocratic in the shallows, or less surely on the rocks, and survey the passing traffic. Dylan Thomas, growing up in Wales, referred to the "heron priested shore...." But for all their dignity, if it is in any sense ecclesiastical, it would remind me more of an elderly Anglican bishop in gaiters and a Norfolk jacket. The lesser white herons are here too, looking innocent and surprised at the presence of other forms of life in their bailiwick.

There is always life on the River and almost always boats as well, perhaps sometimes too many of them. I confess to recognizing no purpose or virtue in the very existence of the Cigarette boat, beloved of our recent president. Their speed is purposeless on the River and their noise is an offense. There is now a law forbidding the playing of loud recorded music from boom boxes in the New York City subways. It was recognized as an unacceptable way of claiming territory that belonged to the whole public, rather like a dog urinating on one's door post to tell the world that he owned the place. The huge explosions of those oversized engines are a sort of acoustical urination, a leg raised for an ejaculation towards the rest of the public to make an unjustified claim on our environment. Besides, they can't possibly use a quarter of the horsepower they carry and stay within the new legal speed limits now in force on the River. Before the Cigarettes there never was a limit in the river.

Not that all the power boats I meet are uniformly dreadful,

and I am not one to use the derisive term "stink pot" to stigmatize what is now a majority of the boat people on the river. Even some of the speedy fellows give evidence of shrewd naval architecture. The pumpkin-seed-shaped bullets of the Bayliner fleet move at great velocity with a minimum of noise and virtually no wake. Their hulls, as is also the case with the Boston Whalers, are skillfully shaped to ride up over the bow wave, flatten it, and skim along on top, planing without moving any great amount of water out of the way as they go. The burly deep-vee sport fishermen, however, can be a real menace to canoe or kayak, and especially to a sailing dinghy running free in light air. When throttled back to a maneuverable speed in the river, those huge hulls cannot plane and they shoulder great waves to both sides as they waddle through the water. Curiously, they produce much larger wakes than the vastly larger tugboats that push the oil barges along at reasonable speed. Just watching all that extravagant horsepower being produced at the expense of many gallons of fuel per hour and resulting mostly in heaping up waves along the shore rather than propelling the boat through the water seems sad and wasteful to me.

By late September and early October the river traffic is confined mostly to the weekends, and not even much of it then. Our final sail of the season was on a Thursday and we were at first entirely alone on the water. It seemed appropriate to conclude the season not with a trip down the river past Essex and Old Lyme, but north, directly into the heart of the country where the first extravagant orange and lemon yellow of the New England autumn was beginning to appear between the green spires of the pine and hemlock.

The wind was moderately strong in the west and the trip upriver was a series of long reaches separated by a few tacks between Selden Creek and Eustasia Island. Along the western side of Selden's Neck, which is really an island, we passed the maintained camp sites that the State Department of Parks looks after. They take reservations for a few limited visits, but the sites are only approachable by boat. Most of the overnighters don't have their own boats but come in canoes rented at the foot of the Gillette Castle State Park. We saw one site occupied with a small tent but no sign of a canoe.

Farther north, just beyond the rocky cleft that is the entrance to Whalebone Cove, we could see the few houses at the Hadlyme Ferry landing. The largest of these, now much remodeled and added to, was once the home of Edith Hamilton and her sisters. The honorary citizen of Athens spent her later years here on the river bank, reading and writing about the reach of the human mind in the far off Greece of twenty-five hundred years ago. The house stands cheek by jowl to the ferry dock, separated from the file of cars waiting for the boat by a low stone wall topped with a thick evergreen hedge. Above both house and dock rises a steep pine clad bluff topped by William Gillette's "castle." Gillette was the actor who originated the role of Sherlock Holmes and made a fortune from it. He built his field stone, three story folly where it commanded a view both up and down the river. There is a two-story living room centered around a great rough stone fire place, a score of stone and ceramic cats built into the walls, carved oak hinges and latches on the doors, and an art gallery on the top floor. We waved at a pair of tourists at the parapet on the terrace, eighty or a hundred feet above us.

The ferryboat that crosses the river here, *Selden III*, is the lineal descendent of boats and barges that have been plying the river at this spot since the later decades of the eighteenth century. A couple of centuries ago it was powered by a horse who walked a treadmill that rolled up a cable from the bottom of the river bed and let it fall again astern as the barge was winched across the river. Today it runs on diesel fuel.

The captain started each traverse of the river by ignoring the upwelling tide. Half way across to the Chester side he would be swept upstream from his goal and then turn to descend upon the docking pilings from the north. The boat shouldered its way into the nest of pilings and held its position against the ramp with engine idling. We had passed behind it when we reached its traverse. The smooth swirl of its wake pushed us farther astern.

North of the ferry crossing, the river swings gently to the west and the file of six or seven riverside hills that Gillette named his house for can be seen. Besides the castle, Gillette constructed a miniature steam railroad that went through his wood land and along the rocky river bank, supported in places by trestles. Gillette was said to entertain his guests by acting the part of the engineer, complete with a denim cap. One of the ironwork arches still survives where his walking trail crossed over the inlets on the shore. It is forlorn and rusted and there seem to be signs posted declaring it unsafe to hikers that might climb past it. There is no sign that the State Department of Parks is thinking about restoring or even preserving it.

I don't think Gillette had any descendants. At least he left his executor free rein as to what to do with the priceless property, only restricting him by the injunction that he should take pains that the place did not fall into the hands of some "blithering sap head who could not tell where he was or by what surrounded." The executor discharged the sacred trust by getting the State to accept the whole property as a park on condition that they would maintain the house from revenues generated by admission fees paid by the curious. It is a lovely park.

We reached on to the north on the freshening west wind. A half mile farther we began to overtake another sailboat following the same course. He was yawl rigged but was sailing without jib or mizzen, much less sail than he could

have been carrying in that
moderate breeze. We over-
hauled him slowly, eventually passing through his lee.
The three in the crew waved
politely and stared hard at
Blueberry. After we passed,
they rolled out a big jib and
caught up to us again. As
they passed, a woman on
the foredeck hailed us.

"Ahoy, *Blueberry*," she
called. "We wanted to see
the name on your transom.
I met you last April in the
checkout line buying boat
gear at Defender in New
Rochelle, and we saw you in
Woodenboat too."

Fame is heady stuff. We
exchanged compliments
about each other's boats and
they soon left us behind.
They had, after all, half again
our water line length and
close to twice our sail area
now that the jib was set.

We pressed on for another half mile to the buoys at the
anchorage of the Middletown Yacht Club. The MYC is in a
pleasant and woodsy location, miles from Middletown. Up
to now I have never sailed farther up the river. But it was time
to stop and turn back down the river. The October daylight
would be almost gone by the time we got back to the Cove
and the evening would be chilly. The next day we would

strike the sails and bring the cabin cushions to the house for winter storage. *Blueberry* herself would be lifted onto the grass beside the yard office at the Cove Landing and set up on poppets, stripped of much of her gear and wrapped in heat-shrunk plastic for the winter.

Across the way from the boat yard I could see that there was neither burgee nor ensign flying from gaff or truck of the Hamburg Cove Yacht Club flag staff. The maples by the Hamburg Community Church were as yellow as *Blueberry*'s boot top. It was time to head for New York or farther south. We had done our sailing for now and it was enough. Only much later on, late next spring, would come a time when the ice would be gone from the river and the green things would be sprouting among the boat yard timbers and cradled hulls. The wonderful yearning to be on the water would return and we would be, like the Rat and the Mole, "up since dawn very busy on matters connected with boats and the opening of the boating season; painting and varnishing, mending paddles, repairing cushions, hunting for missing boathooks, and so on...." So we packed the back of the car with things we couldn't do without in the off season, tied up a few bundles with a couple of yards of old but still fragrant marlin I found in the pocket of a pair of pants I hadn't worn since last spring and drove south down the country road that led to Interstate 95.

Concerning Phil Bolger

I have actually never laid eyes on Philip C. Bolger, nor have I spoken to him. Our business acquaintance has become a friendship entirely through letters. Such relationships were common enough in the eighteenth and nineteenth centuries but much less so today. It is nice to know that we can reach such a level of sympathetic understanding without the contemporary media of telephone, VHF, or fax. He has never seen *Blueberry* in any less abstract form than a photograph, although for one so used to creating three-dimensional beauty on flat sheets of drafting paper, this has been no handicap. He wrote an article about her in *Small Boat Journal* when that late lamented publication flourished: No.66, May 1989.

The reduced size reproductions of the drawings of *Blueberry* are not suitable for construction by a home builder. Full scale plans are available from Phil Bolger or Bernard K. Wolfard at

Common Sense Designs
11765 Ebberts Court
Beaverton, OR 97005

Glossary

Any book about a boat is likely to have quite a lot of nautical vocabulary in it. This is not a matter of putting on airs or lording it over the landspersons who are not in on the mysteries of the elect. There is really no other way to refer to the parts of a boat any more than there are alternatives to words like chin, shin, belly and buttocks when talking about the human body. Sometimes the terms avoid confusion, like port and starboard, which stay the same no matter which way you are facing, while right and left do not. Others, like *wale*, are words of ancient general usage, which have hung on in the conservative parlance of fishermen and sailors while they have lost currency in general speech. I have not listed all of the nautical terms I used since the majority are current in common usage, but those below may help with the technical parts of Chapters III and IV.

Aft This is a direction on a boat and is one of a number of related words that designate things that are on the boat but behind you when you are facing forward. *Abaft* means aft of something else on board. *After* is an adjective designating a location nearer the stern than the bow. *Astern* is a direction of things behind but not on the boat. Phil Bolger gives an example which I paraphrase: "She left her position abaft the main mast and made her way aft to the after deck to look astern."

Beam The greatest breadth of the hull of a boat. This is shortened from the older usage of *Extreme Beam*, the longest transverse timber used in building the vessel.

Boot top A stripe painted at the waterline, or a little above it, separating the anti-fouling paint from the topsides (*q.v.*).

Breaker A small water cask.

Bruce A modern one piece anchor. Originally developed to secure drilling rigs in the stormy waters of the North Sea, very much smaller versions of the patent design have proved to be quite good at holding yachts in a variety of bottom conditions. There is, however, no agreement among experts as to the best sort of anchor. A long rode (*q.v.*) is usually more important than the shape of the hook.

Burgee A pennant, usually triangular, flown to show membership in a yacht club or other boating organization. On a sloop like *Blueberry* it is flown at the masthead while the national ensign is displayed at the tip of the gaff (*q.v.*).

Cavel A corrupt spelling of Kevel (*q.v.*) as Phil Bolger is at pains to point out in Chapter IV.

Chainplates Metal plates bolted to the sides of a vessel to which the shrouds are secured. Since the shrouds hold up the mast and sails against the force of the wind, which can be enormous, the chainplates must be both strong and well fastened to the hull.

Chine The joint between the side and bottom of a boat. In *Blueberry*'s case, the sides and bottom present a fairly sharp angle in cross section at the stern. The angle of the joint grows more obtuse moving forward until it disappears altogether at the bow.

Chine Log The timber to which bottom and side planks are fastened at the chine.

Club A small spar to which the foot of a jib or staysail is fastened to make it behave itself.

Cuddy A small, open-ended shelter at the forward end of the cockpit of a boat too small to have a real cabin.

Deadrise In cross section, the angle the bottom of a boat makes with horizontal (dead flat).

Deadwood The after part of the keel which does not follow the curve of the hull, but continues the line of the greatest depth to form a fin to make the vessel track straight.

Gaff A light, strong spar to which the top edge of a four sided sail is laced. A boat with a mainsail arranged this way is called "gaff rigged," an arrangement more common in the nineteenth and early twentieth centuries than now since yacht racing rules penalize the resulting large mainsail and allow "free" sail area to the large overlapping jibs of rigs with triangular mainsails.

Gallows A frame which supports the boom when the halyards or topping lift are slacked off. It has notches in it to hold the boom steady when tying in a reef. If sturdy enough, it can also protect captain or passengers from being brained during an unexpected jibe. On a vessel as small as *Blueberry* it provides a secure hand-hold when standing on deck or at the helm.

Garboard The bottom plank that forms the joint with the keel. In *Blueberry*'s case the whole bottom is made as a single plywood panel on each side, so the garboard is more of a location than a separate member.

Gooseneck The fitting that joins the boom to the mast. It is double-jointed to allow the boom to swing from side to side as well as up and down.

Horse A transverse rod or wire rope on which the main sheet block rides from side to side when the vessel is put about and the boom swings to the other side.

Keel Apron A stout plank fastened to the top of the keel, inside the hull. It is wider than the keel itself and covers it (like an apron?). The joint between keel and apron turns out to be the location of the rabbet (*q.v.*) that Phil Bolger refers to in Chapter III.

Kevel A large, stout cleat fastened crosswise to a frame or other part of the vessel. It is one of those things that you will recognize when you see it.

Lazarette A storage compartment under the aftermost part of the deck, reached by a hatch, thus separated from the cabin. It would seem to be named for the beggar in Luke (xvi, 20-26) whose presence was kept at a distance in this life although he wound up in the bosom of Abraham later on.

Lazy jacks Lines running from high on the mast to both sides of the boom, branching into one or more inverted "Y"s. They keep the gaff from swinging about and also prevent the sail from getting away from a short handed crew when it is being lowered.

Lee A place protected from the wind. Thus the *leeeside* of the boat is the down wind side. One likes to anchor in the *lee* of an island. *Leeward* is a direction, like *windward*, (*q.v.*) and is for some ancient Anglo Saxon or Dutch reason pronounced *looward*.

LOA Length Over All, as distinguished from Water Line Length. LOA usually does not include the bowsprit (if the boat has one) or the projection of the boom or rudder over the stern. Thus it tells you something about the size of the vessel, but not everything.

Luff The forward edge of a sail. When the boat is sailed too nearly into the wind, this part of the sail begins to quiver and shake first and the boat is said to be luffing. P.C.B. pointed out to me that the forward edge of a gaff sail is often called the *hoist*, but the verb or gerund is the same for all rigs.

MSD The government agencies concerned with toilets on boats coined this usuage. It stands for "Marine Sanitary Device" and spares the verbally fastidious the necessity of ever mentioning toilets in public. Sailors, equally nice about language, usually call the toilet the "head," an ancient usage that comes from the common seamen defecating from a railing below the bowsprit while the officers had a more private closet in the after cabin.

Offsets The distances from a center line or base line where the naval architect locates points on the curved lines that describe the shape of the hull. The *Table of Offsets* thus gives a complete set of points which can be connected by smooth curves to make a pattern for the hull.

Partners Strengthening frameworks around an opening in the deck, especially where the mast goes through the deck.

Rabbet Usually the channel cut into the side of the keel timber to receive the edge of the garboard (*q.v.*). Bolger uses the word to describe the place where the bottom and the keel come together.

Rode   The line attached to an anchor, at least partially comprised of chain as well as a stretchy rope which serves as a spring when the force of wind or wave causes the weight of the hull to pull against the anchor.

Runners   More properly called Running Backstays, these stays are set up to pull back on the masthead. Because of the long boom on gaff rigged (and some Marconi rigged) boats, the lee side runner must be slacked off to allow the boom to swing off the wind. When you come about, you must set up the weather stay. This can be a bother to a short-handed racing crew making many rapid tacks. Surprisingly enough they are little trouble when singlehanding *Blueberry*.

Scantlings   Originally a scantling was a cut off piece of wood. It eventually came to mean the sizes of the various pieces of wood cut up to make the vessel. By now scantlings are the specifications for the size and materials required by the designer.

Sheer   The curve of the deck from bow to stern. Many modern racers have a flat sheer that looks very businesslike but seems to me far less attractive than the traditional curve that kept bow and stern high for seakeeping reasons and let the midships get closer to the water for hauling fish or lobster pots aboard. A few sailboats and lots of power craft have a *reverse sheer* which humps in the middle like the back of a whale. This provides lots of cabin headroom but just doesn't look shippy enough for my taste.

Staysail   Any sail flown aft of the jib, set on one of the stays supporting the mast. Staysail names are determined by the mast that their stay supports. Calling *Blueberry*'s a forestaysail is rather grand, since she has but one mast.

Toe Rails   These are very low bulwarks that are designed to keep things from falling overboard. Although too small to keep the crew from going over the side, their presence gives a remarkable sense of security, knowing that at least your foot won't slip off the deck

Topsides   Not the deck, but the top of the sides, the part above the waterline.

Transom   The flat panel that forms the stern of a flat sterned boat like *Blueberry*. Other sterns could be round (counter sterned) or sharp (canoe sterned or double ended).

Treenails   Pronounced "trunnels," these are actually wooden pegs used to fasten the planks of a vessel to the frames. Not much done these days except where museum vessels are being kept in authentic style.

Vang   A guy rope used to control boom or gaff.

Wale   A plank on the side of a boat that stands out from the rest of the side. This word cames from the same root as *welt*.

Weather   On a boat this word is used not only for the condition of sun, rain or wind, but also as an adjective to identify the side of the vessel upon which the force of the wind is blowing. Bolger's example is "He stood on the weather rail and looked to windward." It can also be used as a verb as in "weathering the rocky point"; that is passing to windward of it.

Windward   The direction the wind or weather is coming from; *cf.* Weather above.

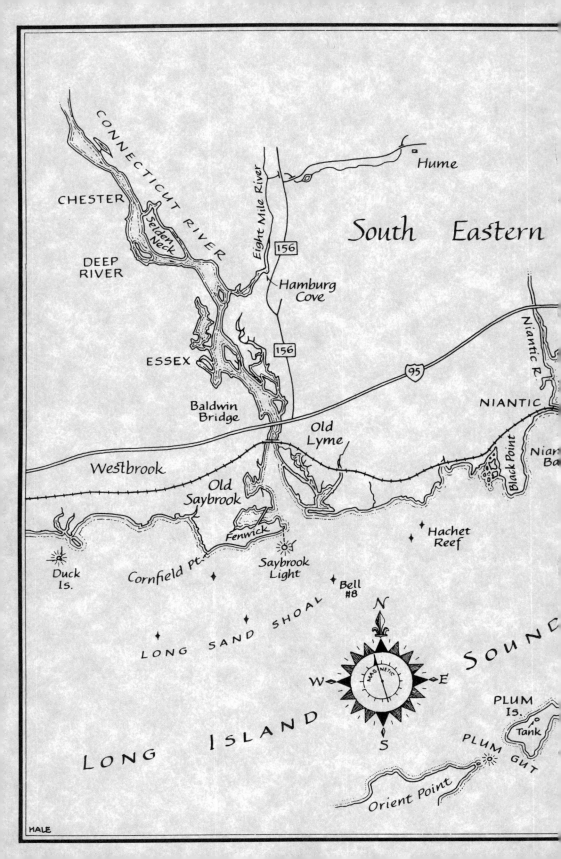